D0883232

JUN 24 2019

A Taste of History

COOKBOOK

ALSO BY CHEF WALTER STAIB

A Sweet Taste of History

The City Tavern Cookbook

Black Forest Cuisine

City Tavern Baking & Dessert Cookbook

A Feast of Freedom

A Taste of History

COOKBOOK

The FLAVORS, PLACES, *and* PEOPLE
that SHAPED AMERICAN CUISINE

CHEF WALTER STAIB

with

MARTHA W. MURPHY
PHOTOGRAPHY BY TODD TRICE

GCC

GRAND CENTRAL
PUBLISHING

NEW YORK   BOSTON

Copyright © 2019 by Walter Staib and Martha W. Murphy
Cover design by Jason Snyder
Cover copyright © 2019 by Hachette Book Group, Inc.

Hachette Book Group supports the right to free expression and the value of copyright.
The purpose of copyright is to encourage writers and artists to produce
the creative works that enrich our culture.

The scanning, uploading, and distribution of this book without permission is a theft
of the author's intellectual property. If you would like permission to use material from
the book (other than for review purposes), please contact permissions@hbgusa.com.
Thank you for your support of the author's rights.

Grand Central Publishing
Hachette Book Group
1290 Avenue of the Americas, New York, NY 10104
grandcentralpublishing.com
twitter.com/grandcentralpub

First edition: May 2019

Grand Central Publishing is a division of Hachette Book Group, Inc.
The Grand Central Publishing name and logo is a trademark of Hachette Book Group, Inc.

The publisher is not responsible for websites (or their content) that are not owned by the publisher.

The Hachette Speakers Bureau provides a wide range of authors for speaking events.
To find out more, go to www.hachettespeakersbureau.com or call (866) 376-6591.

Photography by Todd Trice
Food styled by Chef Walter Staib
Print book interior design by Jason Snyder

Library of Congress Cataloging-in-Publication Data

Names: Staib, Walter, author. | Murphy, Martha W., 1951– author.
Title: A taste of history cookbook : the flavors, places, and people that
shaped American cuisine / Chef Walter Staib with Martha W. Murphy.
Description: New York : Grand Central Publishing, 2019. | Includes index.
Identifiers: LCCN 2018051065| ISBN 9781538746684 (hardcover) | ISBN
9781538746677 (ebook)
Subjects: LCSH: Cooking, American. | LCGFT: Cookbooks.
Classification: LCC TX715 .S775345 2019 | DDC 641.5973—dc23
LC record available at https://lccn.loc.gov/2018051065

ISBNs: 978-1-5387-4668-4 (hardcover), 978-1-5387-4667-7 (ebook)

Printed in the United States of America

WOR

10 9 8 7 6 5 4 3 2 1

To my dearest Gloria

CONTENTS

INTRODUCTION

From Many, We Are One

✦──➤─✳──➤─✦

THE FORMATION OF A DEMOCRACY AND AMERICA'S CUISINE

In this cookbook, you will find recipes for the dishes that you have seen on my television program, *A Taste of History*, complete with detailed step-by-step instructions, ingredients, and measurements that will allow you to successfully re-create delicious, historic fare in your own kitchen. And you won't need a hearth with burning hardwood logs—the recipes have all been tested with modern equipment and then retested to ensure that you will get eighteenth-century results in the comfort of your own home. Each recipe also indicates the show that featured it so that you can revisit (or watch for the first time) how each dish was made 250-plus years ago.

Avid fans of *A Taste of History* will notice that I couldn't tackle *every* recipe they've seen on the show. If we'd included the hundreds of dishes that have been prepared over the years, you'd be holding several encyclopedia-size volumes. Plus, I took into account the availability

of ingredients: while I may have the luxury of traveling to Malaysia or Guyana to prepare historic fare, I understand that very few people travel across oceans to complete their shopping trips. I want home cooks to see that these

amazing dishes, while rooted in the past, can find a place on today's table.

That said, you may find dishes here that call for ingredients you have never used, such as tongue, or calves' feet, or tripe. I encourage you to try them! Our forebears were frugal and inventive cooks, as you know from watching *A Taste of History* and will learn in the pages that follow. The colonists used every part of the animal and every bit of the plant that they could. This is not to say eighteenth-century dining was a slog; to the contrary, it was a delight, a highlight of the day, as the beautiful and delicious dishes these recipes yield will show you and your guests again and again.

You will also learn a bit about the immigrants who came here and the culinary traditions they brought with them. Our nation has been shaped by them, both our democracy and our cuisine. The United States has often been referred to as a melting pot because of the diverse countries of origin of its people. *E Pluribus Unum,* first used on the Great Seal of the United States in 1782 and which means "From Many, We Are One," reflects that truth. It is one that is deeply meaningful to me, and that I believe we should all be proud of.

This book is a project I have long envisioned—the culmination of many years operating City Tavern in Old City Philadelphia and my knowledge of authentic historic cuisine. City Tavern is a landmark building that originally opened its doors to the public

in 1773. When I took over operation of this grand building in 1994, my goal was to create a truly authentic eighteenth-century dining experience. The restaurant has become both my test kitchen and office; it's here that I spend hours perfecting recipes or diving into research. Fortunately, the building is part of the National Park Service, and through this relationship I have been granted access to records and historical documents that would otherwise be unreachable. Through their files and the assistance of the PhDs and other geniuses that are a part of this wonderful organization, I was able to build City Tavern into *the* destination for colonial fare—the restaurant I'd always dreamed of.

City Tavern had been a local hotspot long before I stepped into its kitchens. The National Park Service's records included Benjamin Franklin's newspaper the *Pennsylvania Gazette,* which featured a fascinating social column. It detailed the events in high-society Philadelphia, and City Tavern was often mentioned as *the* venue in the colonies. It was not just the site where Franklin would drink ale; it was where Washington and Lafayette started their lifelong friendship, and it was the setting for the treasonous meetings of the Continental Congress!

I wasn't the only one with a passion for historical accuracy when it came to City Tavern—the National Park Service spent a total of twenty years doing painstaking

research to ensure the historical accuracy of the building. Every detail had to be researched, from the colors of curtains to the carving style of the crown molding.

Even with the help of the team at the National Park Service, we encountered many surprises as we immersed ourselves in the historical accuracy of the building and of our menu. Yet at the same time, it felt oddly familiar. The Mid-Atlantic region during the colonial period had a very heavy German presence. Being a German-born American, I immediately felt at home with the food of this period. The old-world traditions I had learned watching my relatives when I was growing up were not considered old world; there was an unbroken link of tradition going back to antiquity. This was not a throwback to another time, it was just how things were done, which is why the line between historical and "modern" food has always been blurred in my mind.

In addition, many of the recipes and techniques that I discovered during my research for City Tavern were the same that I had learned as a young man beginning my career at Hotel Post in Nagold, located in the heart of the Black Forest in Germany. Hotel Post, a European landmark, opened in 1773—the same year as City Tavern! Hotel Post hosted heads of state and other famous figures in Europe, such as Napoleon himself, at the same time that City Tavern was providing Madeira and meals to George Washington and Thomas Jefferson. The parallels were uncanny. It was as if I'd been preparing for *A Taste of History*, and in turn, this book, my whole life.

When I began the television show, *A Taste of History* was a unique concept; there was no guarantee that the public would respond. It wasn't your typical cooking show—I questioned if people would be interested in a program that spanned the gap between historical documentary and a cooking program, one that shows the labor, techniques, and finesse of cooking in the eighteenth-century manner. I needed to start the series with a bang. So I delved into the genius of Ben Franklin; the story of Washington's chef, Hercules; and, the pièce de résistance, an epic four-part episode filmed at Monticello. I was able to cook in the kitchen of Jefferson, an opportunity that had not been granted before—nor has it since.

It took a monumental effort to make that first season happen and I was thrilled to have received such a positive response from viewers as well as the Academy of Television Arts & Sciences with my very first Emmy. There were more to come in the years that followed, and while I am very proud of the awards the show has won, I'm always moved when I hear from the viewers themselves—other like-minded food-lovers who have reignited their passion for the history of our nation and the culinary arts.

I am on-site at City Tavern every day (unless filming abroad), so I often have the wonderful opportunity to speak with our guests personally. I have received countless requests for this cookbook, which is my seventh to date, and I am honored to share it with you.

All of the photographs in this book feature not only authentic recipes but also the actual china on which our Founding Fathers may have dined! With those visuals and the dishes they may inspire you to create, I hope you will enjoy the escapism and education of cooking your way through *A Taste of History*.

After all, it is for *you* that I have written this book. This book features the figures that helped shape America's history, the places that inspired them, and the flavors that have become quintessentially American. But history does not stop. It is happening every day and is kept alive by enthusiasm. I am doing my part and I know that you, the reader and viewer, will do yours as well.

—*Walter Staib*

1

APPETIZERS

From Fritters to Terrine

ppetizers were not commonly part of a meal in eighteenth-century America, at least not as we think of appetizers today. Inviting friends over for a casual evening of drinks and "small plates" was simply not done in America's early days. And starting a dinner party with a single item as a first course—something we regularly do today—would have been a strange sight on an eighteenth-century table.

While cookbooks from this era do not identify "appetizers" as a distinct category for recipes, we do know that in well-to-do households of the eighteenth century entertaining called for extravagant dinners of many courses with multiple dishes per course. My research for *A Taste of History* has yielded a wealth of recipes that can stand alone as modern-day appetizers or first courses.

In this chapter, you'll find delicious dishes to use when entertaining—whether you are hosting a small intimate gathering or a large celebration. In some cases, after you've tried a recipe here as part of a "drinks and small plates" menu, you may decide to use it for a light, weeknight family dinner—just add a green salad and you're done.

I've offered some context for each recipe in the headnotes that fans of *A Taste of History* will surely enjoy—these factoids and stories should come in handy at any dinner party. Your guests will get a kick out of learning the history behind the dishes. You can even kick off the evening with a fun toast to the men and women who helped shape our democracy.

The recipes I selected for this chapter include dishes you are likely familiar with, such as Baked Stuffed Clams, as well as ones that highlight more unusual ingredients like kohlrabi, beef tongue, calves' feet, conch, and venison. I did this to expand your repertoire and because these dishes and ingredients were popular in eighteenth-century America. When you make, serve, and enjoy these less-familiar foods, you will be experiencing a true taste of history and, I hope, realizing that trying foods that are new to you and your family is a worthwhile adventure.

Some of these dishes are served hot, some are served chilled, and some at room temperature. In many recipes, you'll find you can prepare parts in advance. Also note that some call for frying an ingredient in hot oil; be sure to use a cooking thermometer so that the oil has reached and is kept at the proper temperature. Oil that is not hot enough can result in a soggy finish, while oil that is too hot will burn the batter.

Mussels and Artichokes

Shrimp Toast

Stuffed Kohlrabi

Pickled Beef Tongue Salad

*Lobster and Corn Galettes
with Spicy Tomato Relish*

Snapper Ceviche

Fried Asparagus with Herbed Rémoulade

Exuma Conch Fritters with Calypso Sauce

Oysters Doré with Béchamel Sauce

Fried Calves' Feet

Scallops Croustillant with Saffron Sauce

Asparagus and Oyster Ragoût

Baked Stuffed Clams

Venison Terrine

MUSSELS and ARTICHOKES

SERVES 6 TO 8

A FEW YEARS AGO, while in France filming an episode, I had the once-in-a-lifetime opportunity to be present for the installation of the last cannon on *L'Hermione*—a replica of the frigate General Lafayette sailed to America in 1780 to support the colonists' cause.

This journey of Lafayette's was his second trip to the New World; just a few years prior to his journey on the *L'Hermione*, he had met with George Washington for the very first time right at my establishment in Philadelphia, City Tavern. In the ballroom on the second floor (known as the Long Room) Lafayette spoke with Washington on August 5, 1777, to pledge his service to the revolution. I feel incredibly fortunate to have such a close connection to this moment in history, and I am very proud that guests can still enjoy the very same room to this day while joining us for a meal.

L'Hermione's home port, Rochefort, France, includes a beautiful open-air market. Inspired by the seafood and produce there, I created this recipe to pay homage to the story of the ship and the men who sailed on it. I include barley as a tribute to the colonists, who considered it a staple. Before *L'Hermione* set sail to retrace its original trans-Atlantic journey, I was deeply honored to be named its culinary ambassador.

- 4 artichokes
- ½ lemon
- Kosher salt
- Olive oil, for sautéing
- 2 garlic cloves, coarsely chopped
- 1 pound live mussels, cleaned
- 2 cups dry white wine
- 2 large heirloom tomatoes, diced
- 1 bunch pencil-thin asparagus, tips only
- 2 tablespoons fresh tarragon leaves
- 2 tablespoons chopped fresh chives
- ⅓ cup rice vinegar
- 2 cups cooked barley (al dente)

- Freshly grated white pepper
- Freshly grated nutmeg, to taste
- 3 scallions, chopped
- 1 cup yellow or red cherry tomatoes, halved, for garnish

In a large stockpot, bring 2 quarts water to a boil and reduce to a simmer over low heat. Using a serrated knife, cut about an inch off the top of each artichoke and trim the end of the stems even with the base of the artichoke; as you work, rub each with the lemon half to prevent oxidizing. Place them in the simmering water with a dash of salt and cook until tender, about 20 minutes. With a slotted spoon, transfer the artichokes to a plate.

When they are cool enough to handle, remove and discard the outer leaves. Using a small spoon, remove and discard the choke. What remains is the artichoke heart. Cut each heart into eight pieces and set aside.

Coat a large saucepan with a thin film of olive oil and set it over medium heat. When the oil is hot but not smoking, add the garlic, then the mussels and white wine. Give it a quick stir and then simmer, uncovered, for 15 minutes, or until the mussel shells have opened. Remove the pan from the heat and use a slotted spoon to transfer the mussels to a plate. When they are cool enough to handle, remove the mussels from their shells; reserve a few shells for garnish.

To assemble: Combine the diced heirloom tomatoes, asparagus tips, tarragon, and chives in a large bowl. Add ½ cup olive oil and the vinegar and toss lightly; let stand for 10 minutes to allow the flavors to marry. Add the artichokes and barley. Season with salt, pepper, and nutmeg. Sprinkle the scallions over the top, add the mussels, and toss to combine.

Transfer the mixture to a serving bowl and garnish with a few mussel shells, if desired, and the cherry tomatoes. Serve immediately.

CHEF's NOTES

- ❧ You can tell an **artichoke** is cooked when the bottom leaves are easily removed. As a shortcut, purchase artichoke hearts (in cans or jars) at your grocery store.

- ❧ Be sure to *carefully* examine the **live mussels** to ensure that each is firmly closed before cooking. Any opening of the shell, regardless of how slight, means that the mussel is no longer fresh and would be dangerous to consume.

- ❧ When cooking **barley,** the best level of doneness is al dente. It loses its pleasantly chewy texture if overcooked.

To watch a demonstration of how this recipe is made, and to learn more about the history of eighteenth-century America, see Season 6, Episode 610.

SHRIMP TOAST

SERVES 6

THE COLONIAL RECIPE FOR this dish was called "To Butter Shrimps," and it was most often served over a *sippet*, the colonial term for fried bread. Versions of "buttered shrimp" recipes from this era vary widely; Martha Washington's called simply for shrimp, butter, and pepper. This recipe more closely follows the elegant version found in Eliza Smith's *The Compleat Housewife: Or Accomplished Gentlewoman's Companion*—printed in 1742, it was the first cookbook published in the colonies.

For this recipe, I like to use a quality bread that is slightly stale. I purchase a loaf of bread and leave it out for a day, a step that makes it firm enough to maintain its form.

- 2¼ cups all-purpose flour
- 3 eggs, beaten
- 2¼ cups whole milk
- 1½ tablespoons clarified butter (see Chef's Note, page 17) or olive oil
- 1 tablespoon finely chopped fresh basil
- 1 tablespoon finely chopped fresh parsley, plus more for garnish
- 1 tablespoon finely chopped fresh thyme leaves
- 1 tablespoon finely chopped fresh chives
- Pinch of freshly grated nutmeg
- Pinch of kosher salt
- Pinch of freshly ground white pepper
- 8 tablespoons (1 stick) unsalted butter
- 6 slices Sally Lunn Bread (page 194) or other fine-crumb bread, cut 1½ inches thick (see Chef's Notes)
- 1 garlic clove, minced

- 1 small shallot, minced
- 1½ pounds extra-small shrimp, shelled and deveined
- ¼ cup dry white wine, such as Sauvignon Blanc
- 1 cup Béchamel Sauce (page 248), warmed

In a large mixing bowl, whisk together the flour, eggs, milk, clarified butter, basil, parsley, thyme, chives, nutmeg, salt, and pepper.

Heat 6 tablespoons of the butter in a large skillet over medium heat. Dip the bread slices into the batter, place in the pan, and cook until both sides are well browned, about 3 minutes per side. Remove from skillet and keep warm.

Heat the remaining 2 tablespoons butter in a separate pan over medium heat. Add the garlic and shallot and sauté for approximately 3 minutes, or until translucent but not browned. Add the shrimp and sauté for 3 to 5 minutes, until they are completely pink.

Add the wine to deglaze the pan, loosening any browned bits on the bottom of the pan with a wooden spoon. Cook for approximately 3 minutes, or until the wine is reduced by half.

Stir in the béchamel and remove from the heat.

Using a cookie/biscuit cutter or tip of a knife, cut a 2-inch-diameter round hole from the center of each piece of bread; place a slice of bread on individual plates. Spoon a portion of the shrimp mixture into each hole, being sure to dribble a little sauce over the rest of the slice. Lean the toasted bread cut-out at an angle on the shrimp and sprinkle each serving with parsley. Serve immediately.

CHEF'S NOTES

❦ It is important to use a **serrated knife** when cutting bread. A smooth blade will crush a loaf of bread, whereas the saw-like blade of a serrated knife will not.

❦ Making the **toast** is very similar to making French toast. I recommend that you use a well-seasoned cast-iron skillet or a nonstick skillet; it is impossible to finish this recipe successfully if the toast sticks to the pan.

See Season 2, Episode 204

STUFFED KOHLRABI

SERVES 6

FOR THOSE NOT FAMILIAR with this exotic-named vegetable, kohlrabi is part of the cabbage family. It has gained in popularity recently, thanks in part to its versatility. The name is of German root: *kohl* means "cabbage" and *rabi* means "turnip." When I was growing up in the Black Forest, kohlrabi was a staple on our family dinner table. Since I was familiar with kohlrabi as a popular German food, I was not surprised to find that the Amish and Pennsylvania Dutch planted and used kohlrabi regularly in the eighteenth century. It was not just the settlers with German heritage, however, who enjoyed this nutritious vegetable; Mount Vernon's kitchen garden boasted a healthy supply of kohlrabi, and it was a mainstay at Monticello as well.

One of the valuable aspects of kohlrabi is its ease of cultivation; it is one of the fastest growing members of the cabbage family, and it can be left in the field until just before the first frost, after which it can survive the rest of the winter perfectly in a root cellar. All of these features would have appealed to the colonists.

- 6 medium-large kohlrabi
- Kosher salt
- Olive oil, for sautéing
- 1 large white onion, finely diced
- 3 garlic cloves, minced
- 2 pounds ground lamb, beef, or pork
- 3 eggs
- 2 cups fine fresh bread crumbs
- 2 tablespoons chopped fresh parsley
- ⅛ teaspoon freshly grated nutmeg
- Freshly ground black pepper
- Pinch of paprika
- 1½ cups grated Gruyère cheese

Preheat oven to 350°F.

Hollow out each kohlrabi to create a bowl, leaving the walls and bottom about ¼ inch thick; set aside along with the scooped-out flesh.

Bring a large stockpot of lightly salted water to a boil. Carefully place the hollowed-out kohlrabi in the water and simmer until fork tender, about 15 minutes; do not overcook. Transfer with a slotted spoon to a plate to cool completely.

Heat a small amount of olive oil in a large skillet set over medium heat. Add the onion and garlic and sauté until translucent, but not browned. Remove from the pan and allow to cool.

Finely chop the reserved kohlrabi flesh. In a medium bowl, combine the kohlrabi with the cooled onion and garlic, the lamb (or beef or pork), eggs, bread crumbs, parsley, and nutmeg. Mix to combine thoroughly.

Sauté a tablespoon of the meat mixture and taste for seasoning; adjust as necessary with salt and pepper.

Fill the cooled kohlrabi shells with the meat mixture, top with the shredded Gruyère, and dust the tops with paprika. Place in a roasting pan and bake for 45 minutes or until the cheese is nicely browned. Serve immediately.

CHEF'S NOTE

- As you are preparing the **kohlrabi,** it is important to cut the bottom evenly so that it will sit upright during the baking process. An uneven bottom can cause it to tip over and spill the contents while in the oven.

See Season 9, Episode 910

PICKLED BEEF TONGUE SALAD

SERVES 4 TO 6

BEEF TONGUE IS NOW considered an exotic cut of meat by most, and I'm aware that many modern home cooks may shy away from a recipe with tongue as the star. This was not always the case. Beef tongue was available and purchased frequently in local butcher shops until just a few decades ago.

In the eighteenth century, beef tongue was considered a delicacy. Its subtle flavor and velvety texture were enjoyed on special occasions. Never willing to waste a single part of the cow after the slaughter, eighteenth-century cooks developed many recipes for beef tongue. It was pickled, roasted, stuffed, stewed, potted, and even rubbed with charcoal to preserve it in the same manner as Westphalia ham.

- ♥ 14 ounces pickled beef tongue, cut into thin slices and julienned
- ♥ 2 large dill pickles, halved lengthwise and then sliced thinly into half-moons
- ♥ 1 red onion, halved from root to stem and then sliced thinly into half-moons
- ♥ 6 medium watermelon radishes (4 julienned; 2 cut into half-moon slices for garnish)
- ♥ 2 garlic cloves, finely minced
- ♥ ¼ cup chopped fresh chives
- ♥ ¼ cup rice vinegar
- ♥ ¼ cup olive oil
- ♥ 1 tablespoon finely chopped fresh parsley
- ♥ Kosher salt and freshly ground black pepper
- ♥ Red leaf lettuce leaves

In a large bowl, combine the beef tongue with the pickle slices, red onion, julienned radishes, garlic, and chives. Toss together gently. Add the vinegar, oil, and parsley and toss again. Season to taste with salt and pepper. Serve immediately on a platter over a bed of tender lettuce and garnish with the radish slices.

CHEF'S NOTES

- ♥ While **pickled beef tongue** was widely available at one point, it is now considered a specialty item. The best source today will be Jewish delis or butcher shops.
- ♥ **Watermelon radishes** not available? Any variety of radish may be used for this recipe. The crisp sharpness of any radish blends perfectly with pickled beef tongue.

See Season 7, Episode 706

LOBSTER AND CORN GALETTES WITH SPICY TOMATO RELISH

SERVES 4

LOBSTERS ARE AN EXPENSIVE item today, and usually reserved for celebratory occasions. In the eighteenth century, however, lobsters were not a popular item on most menus. Readily available up and down the Eastern Seaboard, they were considered poor man's food. In fact, in the eighteenth century lobsters were served to prisoners so often that there were prison riots, which led to legislation that the crustacean could be served to prisoners no more than a few times a week.

- ⅓ cup finely diced peeled Yukon Gold potato (1 potato)
- 1 teaspoon olive oil
- 2 tablespoons finely chopped onion
- 1 cup all-purpose flour
- ¼ teaspoon baking powder
- 1 egg, beaten
- 1 cup whole milk
- 1 tablespoon clarified butter (see Chef's Note, page 17) or olive oil
- 1 tablespoon finely chopped fresh basil
- 1 tablespoon finely chopped fresh parsley
- 1 teaspoon finely chopped fresh thyme leaves
- 1 tablespoon finely chopped fresh chives
- Pinch of freshly grated nutmeg
- ⅛ teaspoon kosher salt
- ⅛ teaspoon freshly ground white pepper
- 2 ears white corn, grilled, then kernels cut from the cob

- 1 pound cooked lobster meat, diced (from a 1½- to 2-pound live lobster, if you are cooking it yourself)
- 4 tablespoons unsalted butter
- Spicy Tomato Relish (recipe follows)
- Microgreens, for garnish

Bring a medium stockpot of lightly salted water to a boil. Add the diced potato and cook just until al dente, checking for doneness after 2 minutes. Drain and set aside to cool completely.

In a small skillet, heat the oil over medium heat until hot but not smoking. Add the onion and sauté until translucent; set aside to cool completely.

Combine the flour, baking powder, egg, milk, clarified butter (or olive oil), basil, parsley, thyme, chives, nutmeg, salt, and pepper in a large mixing bowl, whisking until smooth. Gently fold in the cooked potatoes and onions, along with the corn and lobster.

Melt the 4 tablespoons butter in a large nonstick skillet over medium heat. In batches, drop the lobster/potato mixture into the hot butter by the tablespoonful (each should result in a 2-inch fritter). Cook for 1 to 2 minutes per side, until golden brown. Transfer to a platter lined with paper towels to absorb any excess oil. Repeat until the mixture is used up.

To serve, place three galettes on each plate along with a spoonful of the Spicy Tomato Relish. Garnish with microgreens.

CHEF'S NOTE

❧ The **corn and potato** are a major part of what makes this recipe so good. It is very important to avoid overcooking them as it will adversely affect the texture of the galettes and dull the rich flavors of both ingredients.

See Season 2, Episode 209

SPICY TOMATO RELISH

Makes 2 cups

- ❧ 4 large plum tomatoes, deseeded and diced
- ❧ ¼ cup chopped red onion
- ❧ 2 ounces white balsamic vinegar
- ❧ ¼ teaspoon crushed red pepper flakes
- ❧ ¼ teaspoon chopped garlic
- ❧ ¼ teaspoon chopped fresh basil
- ❧ ¼ teaspoon freshly ground black pepper
- ❧ ⅛ teaspoon Kosher salt

Combine the tomatoes, red onion, vinegar, red pepper, garlic, basil, pepper, and salt in a large mixing bowl. Allow flavors to meld at room temperature for 15 minutes before serving.

SNAPPER CEVICHE

SERVES 4 TO 6

CEVICHE IS A REFRESHING seafood dish that has been enjoyed for centuries in Latin America, but one that has only gained popularity in America since the 1980s. The modern version originated in Peru, although the roots of the dish go back much further: The Spaniards brought citrus fruit to the New World during their explorations. It is commonly believed that similar Moorish dishes, enjoyed at the time in Spain, played a major role in the development of ceviche in Peru.

Ceviche is traditionally made from fresh raw fish marinated in citrus juices and spiced with chili peppers. The acid from limes and lemons changes the structure of the proteins in the fish, essentially "cooking" it without heat.

Ceviche is now popular all over the world, but especially so in the Caribbean. When I was in Ocho Rios, Jamaica, making this dish for *A Taste of History*, I splashed in some twenty-one-year-old spiced rum (we were in Jamaica!)—it added incredible depth and flavor. Tequila may also be used as a flavor enhancer in place of the rum.

- 1 pound skinless red snapper fillets, cut into ¼-inch dice
- ¾ cup fresh sibble (sour) orange juice (or see Chef's Notes for substitute)
- ¼ cup fresh lemon juice (2 lemons), optional
- ⅛ habanero or Scotch Bonnet chili pepper, seeded and minced
- ½ cup thinly julienned red bell pepper
- ½ cup thinly julienned yellow bell pepper
- ½ cup thinly julienned red onion
- 1 garlic clove, finely minced
- 1 teaspoon ground allspice
- 1 tablespoon minced fresh cilantro
- Kosher salt
- 1 tablespoon extra-virgin olive oil
- Splash (about ½ teaspoon) Jamaican rum or tequila, optional
- Breadfruit chips (sweet potato or taro chips can also be used)

In a large bowl, toss the diced fish with the sibble orange juice, lemon juice (if using), chili pepper, red and yellow bell peppers, red onion, garlic, allspice, and half the cilantro; season with a little salt. Cover and refrigerate the snapper ceviche for 30 minutes.

Stir in the remaining cilantro and drizzle with extra virgin olive oil. Add a splash of rum (or tequila) if you like. Serve immediately with crispy breadfruit chips.

See Season 7, Episode 710

─── CHEF'S NOTES ───

❧ When preparing ceviche, it is imperative that you **use only the freshest fish** from your local fishmonger, as the citric acid is the only "cooking" element.

❧ This recipe calls for **sibble (sour or bitter) oranges** for the acidic base. For those living in areas where sour oranges are not available, add liberal amounts of lemon or lime juice (or both) to orange juice.

❧ The heat factor of chili peppers is measured by Scoville heat units. A jalapeño has 80,000 Scoville heat units, while a **habanero** (also known as **Scotch Bonnet chili**) from Jamaica or Mexico's Yucatan Peninsula has been found to have 550,000 Scoville heat units. Always wear rubber gloves when handling this fiery pepper!

FRIED ASPARAGUS with HERBED RÉMOULADE

SERVES 6

ASPARAGUS WAS A COMMON and widely liked vegetable in colonial times. In his *Garden Book*, Thomas Jefferson mentions numerous plantings of asparagus between 1767 and 1816. In his notes for the President's House, he included instructions for frying asparagus—but it was placed in the list of desserts. A mistake? Although no exact recipe survives, surely asparagus would have been served as a first or second course dish at Monticello.

Whether or not Thomas Jefferson intended it as a dessert, my asparagus dish is on the savory side and uses one of Jefferson's favorite herbs: tarragon. Today, tarragon is not as popular as it was in eighteenth-century cooking, but I still use it daily at City Tavern. It provides a sophisticated and subtle flavor that Jefferson liked to describe as "soft."

- 1½ pounds asparagus, peeled and trimmed
- 2¼ cups all-purpose flour
- 3 eggs, beaten
- 1¼ cups whole milk
- 1½ tablespoons clarified butter (see Chef's Notes) or olive oil
- 1 tablespoon fresh tarragon leaves (*not* chopped)
- ⅛ teaspoon freshly grated nutmeg
- ⅛ teaspoon kosher salt
- ⅛ teaspoon freshly ground white pepper
- 4 cups vegetable oil, for frying
- 1 cup Herbed Rémoulade (page 262)

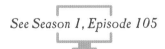

See Season 1, Episode 105

In a stockpot, bring 2 quarts of lightly salted water to a boil; drop in the asparagus and cook until just tender, 2 to 3 minutes. Lift the asparagus out with tongs and immediately place in a pan of ice water to stop the cooking. Let stand for 5 minutes, drain, and pat dry with towels. Set the asparagus aside.

In a large mixing bowl, whisk together the flour, eggs, milk, clarified butter (or olive oil), tarragon, nutmeg, salt, and pepper.

Heat the oil in a deep-fryer or 4-quart heavy saucepan over high heat to 350°F. Dip the asparagus in the batter, shaking off any excess, then carefully drop the spears into the hot oil a few at a time. Fry until golden brown, about 2 minutes. Use a slotted spoon to remove the asparagus from the oil and place on a baking sheet lined with paper towels to absorb any excess oil. Continue until all pieces are fried.

Place the asparagus on a platter with the rémoulade on the side and serve immediately.

CHEF'S NOTES

❦ Because it is free of milk solids, **clarified butter** has a higher smoking point than regular butter (meaning it doesn't burn as quickly), has a longer shelf life, and a lighter flavor. It is also called ghee and is available at most grocery stores. But it is easy to make: Melt unsalted butter in a saucepan and gently simmer on low heat until the white milk solids have settled on the bottom of the pan and the clear, clarified butter remains on top. Skim off and discard any foam that rises to the surface, then carefully pour the clarified butter into a jar, leaving the solids behind, and store in the refrigerator for up to four weeks.

❦ **Tarragon** is available in supermarkets, dried and fresh. For this recipe, I recommend that you use fresh tarragon (if you use dried, reduce the amount to ½ teaspoon). *Do not chop fresh tarragon.* Chopping can bruise the herb as well as increase the chance of accidentally including some of the stem, which has a woody texture and is not a pleasant addition. Instead, gently pull the tarragon leaves from the stem with your fingers and use whole for best results.

EXUMA CONCH FRITTERS with CALYPSO SAUCE

SERVES 4 TO 6

WHILE THE CARIBBEAN ISLANDS bring to mind lush, tropical jungles teeming with life and rich volcanic soil, nothing could be further from the truth in the case of Exuma. This island, while beautiful, has the ominous nickname: The Island Where Nothing Grows. The salty soil and water created a very successful salt-raking industry in the eighteenth century, but this natural feature greatly limited crop production. Luckily, conch has always been plentiful in the waters surrounding Exuma and was enjoyed by residents of Exuma even before European contact.

This conch fritter captures the true essence of Exuma's cuisine. In the Bahamas, cooks use fresh conch to make fritters, and they remove the meat from the shell themselves. But if conch is not readily available, you can make the fritters by using chopped conch meat purchased from a fish market.

FOR THE FRITTERS

- 1 quart vegetable oil, for frying
- ¾ cup all-purpose flour
- 1 sprig fresh thyme leaves
- Kosher salt and freshly ground black pepper
- 1 cup chopped conch meat
- ½ onion, chopped
- ½ green bell pepper, chopped
- 2 stalks celery, chopped
- 1 teaspoon tomato paste
- 1 cup water

FOR THE CALYPSO SAUCE

- ¼ cup ketchup
- Juice of 4 limes
- 2 tablespoons mayonnaise
- 2 tablespoons hot sauce
- Kosher salt and freshly ground black pepper

Make the fritters: Heat the oil in a large heavy-bottomed saucepan, Dutch oven, or deep fryer to 365°F.

In a large mixing bowl, combine the flour, thyme, salt, and pepper. Mix in the conch meat, onion, bell pepper, celery, tomato paste, and water.

In batches, drop the batter by rounded tablespoons into the hot oil and fry until golden brown. Use a slotted spoon to transfer the fritters to a baking sheet lined with paper towels to absorb any excess oil.

Make the sauce: In a small bowl, mix the ketchup, lime juice, mayonnaise, hot sauce, salt, and pepper. Serve the sauce on the side with the fritters.

CHEF'S NOTE

- If **conch** meat is not available, try using shrimp, as it is an excellent substitute.

See Season 3, Episode 312

OYSTERS DORÉ with BÉCHAMEL SAUCE

SERVES 8

WHEN WE'RE NOT FILMING on location, *A Taste of History*'s home studio is the handsome Harriton House in Bryn Mawr, a short distance from Philadelphia. Built in 1704, this stately stone structure was the home of Charles Thomson, a major name in the eighteenth century. Thomson's most famous work was the design of the Presidential Seal of the United States of America.

Thomas Jefferson and Charles Thomson were close friends, and whenever in town, Jefferson was known to spend a good deal of time at Harriton House. When archaeologists surveyed the property in the 1970s, they recovered a substantial number of oyster shells in the area around the home. While oysters were enjoyed by many in the eighteenth century, it is reasonable to believe that Jefferson's insatiable appetite for them helped contribute to this trove.

While Jefferson's favorite oyster dish is not known, I have chosen this recipe as an homage to his love of oysters and fondness for French cuisine. *Doré* is a quintessential French technique: here, the oysters are egg battered and lightly fried to create a crispy texture on the outside while maintaining the delicate soft interior, complemented with a rich sauce.

- ¼ cup all-purpose flour
- 1 teaspoon paprika
- Pinch of cayenne pepper
- Pinch of kosher salt
- Pinch of freshly ground white pepper
- 24 oysters, purchased shucked with their liquor
- 3 eggs, beaten
- Vegetable oil, as needed, for pan frying the oysters
- 8 tablespoons (1 stick) unsalted butter
- 1 loaf Sally Lunn Bread (page 194) or other fine-crumb bread, sliced into 1½-inch-thick slices
- 1½ cups Béchamel Sauce (page 248)
- 2 tablespoons chopped fresh parsley, for garnish
- Microgreens, for garnish

Season the flour with the paprika, cayenne, salt, and white pepper. Dredge the oysters in the seasoned flour and then dip in the beaten eggs, coating generously.

Coat the bottom of a large frying pan with a little oil and set over medium-high heat. When hot but not smoking, add the oysters in batches without crowding the pan and cook, turning once, until crisp and golden. Oysters cook quickly; be prepared to take them out of the oil a minute after they go in.

In a separate frying pan, melt the butter over medium heat; in batches, add the bread to the pan and toast the slices, flipping once, until golden brown on both sides.

To assemble the dish, place a slice of bread in the center of each plate, spoon 3 tablespoons béchamel onto the bread, and top with 3 fried oysters. Garnish with the parsley and microgreens. Serve immediately.

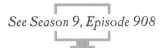

See Season 9, Episode 908

— CHEF'S NOTES —

❦ When **purchasing the oysters** for this recipe, choose the largest ones available. And there is no need to be concerned about the shucking: pre-shucked oysters are readily available and work perfectly for this dish.

❦ Browning **the bread** in butter is an important aspect of this recipe, but thinner slices do not hold up as well. Full loaves of unsliced bread can be hard to find at the supermarket, but your local bakery can probably provide thickly sliced bread or whole loaves. If you choose to take a purist approach to this recipe, baking a loaf of Sally Lunn Bread at home will guarantee you can customize the thickness of the slices.

FRIED CALVES' FEET

SERVES 8

IN HER 1745 COOKBOOK, *The Art of Cookery, Made Plain and Easy*, Hannah Glasse noted that calves' feet were a delicious treat and often part of a special-occasion meal. Although many foods have segued seamlessly from the eighteenth century to the modern world, there are some that have not captured the attention that they deserve. This dish is a prime example.

The eighteenth century was a time of frugality in general, a trait that extended into the kitchen. Waste could not be tolerated when there was no guarantee of successful harvests or livestock. Every part of the animal was used. Calves' feet—in addition to being used in stews and soups or served fried—were prized for the gelatin they provided, which was used to make elaborate molded edible centerpieces for dinner parties in the finest homes.

Fried calves' feet *are* widely enjoyed in other parts of the world to this day. In fact, you will find a version of this recipe on almost every bistro menu in Europe.

- 8 calves' feet, split lengthwise
- 2 carrots, cut into 2-inch segments
- 3 stalks celery, cut into 2-inch segments
- 1 celery root (celeriac), peeled and cut into 2-inch segments
- 1 onion, halved, skin on
- 6 sprigs fresh parsley
- 2 bay leaves
- 1 teaspoon whole peppercorns
- ½ teaspoon whole cloves
- 2 cups all-purpose flour
- Kosher salt and freshly ground black pepper
- ¼ teaspoon fresh grated nutmeg
- 3 to 4 cups fresh bread crumbs
- 3 eggs, beaten
- Lard or vegetable oil, for frying
- 1 lemon, sliced
- ¼ cup chopped fresh chives
- 1 sprig fresh parsley, for garnish
- Herbed Rémoulade (page 262)

Bring a large stockpot of water to a boil; add the calves' feet. Cook at a simmer over low heat for about 1½ hours, or until opaque. Drain the water from the pot, leaving the calves' feet in it. Add the carrots, celery, celery root, onion, parsley, bay leaves, peppercorns, and cloves to the pot and cover with water. Bring to a boil and simmer for 1 hour, or until the outer part of each foot is soft.

Using tongs, remove the calves' feet from stock and set on a platter to cool slightly. *Do not let them cool completely because it will be difficult to remove the cartilage, which is the outer part.* When they have cooled enough to handle, carefully peel the cartilage from the bones with your hands, doing your best not to tear it

off in shreds. Discard the bones or keep to use later in stock.

Pour the flour onto a plate and season with the salt, ground pepper, and nutmeg. Pour the bread crumbs onto a separate plate and pour the eggs into a third dish. One at a time, dredge the calves' feet cartilage in the flour, then dip into the egg, and then into the bread crumbs. Repeat with all of the cartilage.

Meanwhile, heat the lard (or oil) in a large Dutch oven over medium heat to 350°F. In batches if necessary to avoid overcrowding, carefully lower the calves' feet into the hot oil and fry for 7 to 10 minutes, until deep golden brown. Remove from oil with tongs, set briefly on a baking sheet lined with paper towels, and then transfer to a serving platter.

Arrange the lemon slices on the dish and sprinkle chives on top. Garnish with parsley. Serve immediately with the rémoulade.

See Season 3, Episode 308

CHEF'S NOTES

❦ Don't be afraid of this recipe! It may seem a daunting task to procure **calves' feet**, but they are available at specialty food stores, especially Old World–style butcher shops; and most Asian food markets sell them pre-split.

❦ It is very important to **season the flour and not the feet themselves**. The seasoning will not stick while cooking if you apply it directly to the foot and it will result in a bland dish.

❦ Do *not* use panko for the **bread crumbs**. While panko is great for many recipes, this is simply not one of them. Fresh bread crumbs (made at home or from your local bakery) are the only way to go.

SCALLOPS CROUSTILLANT WITH SAFFRON SAUCE

SERVES 6

WHILE FILMING *A TASTE of History*, I was lucky enough to travel to one of the most magical regions of France: Bordeaux. This was where Jefferson fell in love with French wine and created an awareness for the region's namesake red. Before Jefferson "discovered" Bordeaux wine, even the King of France's impressive cellar contained nary a red varietal—a shocking fact to think of today.

I created this recipe with Chef Frédéric at Château Magnol, a sprawling estate in the French countryside. I wanted to include elements from the region that are representative of its beauty and sophistication. The ocean is approximately thirty-three miles away; scallops would have been readily available to the more fortunate at the time, such as Jefferson. The saffron is not just for the taste, but also to celebrate the painstaking process required to harvest the delicate and expensive ingredient. Cookbooks of the colonial era indicate that the English tended to use saffron in sweet dishes, like saffron cake, and to color marzipan. It was the Spanish, and later the French, whose savory saffron recipes began to infiltrate eighteenth-century American cuisine. This dish is a creation that, I hope, would make Jefferson and the French proud.

FOR THE SAFFRON SAUCE

- 1 cup dry white wine
- 2 tablespoons minced shallot
- ⅔ cup heavy cream
- 1 teaspoon saffron
- 3½ tablespoons unsalted butter, cut into small bits
- Kosher salt and freshly ground black pepper

FOR THE CROUSTILLANT

- 6 sheets filo dough
- 1 cup best-quality olive oil
- Kosher salt and freshly ground black pepper
- 16 leaves fresh basil
- 18 scallops (divers' scallops, if possible; see Chef's Notes), freshly shucked
- Olive oil, for sautéing

Make the saffron sauce: Cook the white wine and shallot in a saucepan over medium heat until the liquid is reduced by half, about 10 minutes. Add the cream and saffron and cook for an additional 10 minutes. Whisk in the butter until it is incorporated. Add salt and pepper to taste and set aside.

Make the croustillant: Place one sheet of filo dough on a cutting board and brush with olive oil. Repeat the process with two more sheets, seasoning the top of the third sheet with a little salt and pepper (you will have three stacked sheets of filo). Arrange the basil evenly on top of the third sheet.

Repeat the layering process, topping the basil with three more layered sheets of filo, each one brushed with olive oil (you will now have a stack of six sheets of filo).

Cut the stack of filo in half lengthwise. Thinly slice the scallops horizontally, and arrange them on one of the two halves. Place the other half of stacked filo over the scallops, so the scallops are sandwiched between the two stacks of filo dough. Cut the long sandwich into six equal-size pieces.

Coat the bottom of a large sauté pan with olive oil and place over medium heat. When the oil is hot but not smoking, carefully place the croustillants in the pan. Cook until golden brown on each side (about 3 minutes per side), turning only once.

Set each croustillant on a plate and top with a little saffron sauce. Serve immediately.

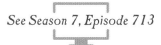

See Season 7, Episode 713

— CHEF'S NOTES —

- If you have not worked with **filo dough** before, note that it is important to keep the dough lightly moistened with olive oil. (Clarified butter will work nicely as an alternative, if preferred.) Should the filo get dry, it will not maintain its shape and it becomes impossible to use. Since filo requires a little finesse, I recommend that you make this recipe (perhaps a half recipe) before you plan to serve it at your dinner party!

- The best **scallops** for this recipe are the U10 size, which just means there are fewer than ten scallops per pound. This size scallop is also known commonly as divers' scallops or sea scallops. The smaller bay scallops are not appropriate for this recipe.

ASPARAGUS and OYSTER RAGOÛT

SERVES 4 TO 6

THIS DISH IS A great example of what the colonists would have enjoyed in the eighteenth century. Asparagus was valued not just for its unique flavor and texture, but also for its early-spring harvest, which was helpful when feeding a family from the garden. Thomas Jefferson wrote about his fondness for asparagus and would anxiously await the moment of harvest on April 8 of every year.

Oysters were plentiful in the eighteenth century all along the Eastern Seaboard, and popular. Philadelphians consumed so many, the shells were used as street paving, for artificial wharves along the Delaware, and even as ballast for ships.

- 1 pound bunch pencil-thin asparagus
- 4 tablespoons unsalted butter
- 1 medium shallot, thinly sliced
- Pinch of kosher salt
- 12 oysters, purchased shucked
- 2 teaspoons turmeric
- 2 to 3 tablespoons Catchup to Last 20 Years (page 246) or fish sauce
- 2 tablespoons chopped fresh chives
- 2 tablespoons chopped fresh parsley

Cut the asparagus into 1- to 1½-inch bite-size pieces.

Heat the butter in a large skillet over medium-high heat. Add the asparagus and shallot with a pinch of salt, lower the heat to medium, and sauté the mix until the shallots are translucent but not browned.

Add the oysters to pan and continue to cook until the edges of the oysters begin to curl, about 1 minute. Add the turmeric and catchup (or fish sauce) and stir to combine. Continue to sauté until the sauce is hot throughout.

Transfer the ragoût to a serving plate, sprinkle with chives and parsley, and serve immediately.

CHEF'S NOTES

- **Asparagus** is sold in bunches that weigh 1 pound, regardless of the thickness of the asparagus. For this recipe, it is my recommendation that you choose the thinnest available asparagus, ideally the circumference of a pencil.
- When purchasing **shucked oysters** for this recipe, the small- to medium-size oysters are ideal.

See Season 7, Episode 701

BAKED STUFFED CLAMS

SERVES 6

ONE CANNOT THINK OF New England cuisine without envisioning one of its most famous staples: the hard-shell clam. Blessed with an abundance of seafood, the coastal communities of New England have consumed a large amount of the ocean's bounty from the very earliest settlements, as they do today. John Adams was particularly fond of clams and it is in his honor that I created this recipe.

- 8 tablespoons (1 stick) unsalted butter
- 12 cherrystone clams, shucked and chopped, shells cleaned and reserved
- 1 red bell pepper, diced small
- 1 green bell pepper, diced small
- 1 medium red onion, diced small
- 8 ounces bacon, one-half diced and one-half cut into 1-inch pieces
- ¼ teaspoon cayenne pepper
- ¼ cup all-purpose flour
- Lemon wedges, for serving

Preheat oven to 400°F.

Melt the butter in a medium skillet over medium heat. Add the clams, peppers, onion, *diced* bacon, and cayenne pepper and cook for about 5 minutes, until the onions and peppers are translucent and tender but not browned. Remove from heat. Stir the flour into the mixture and allow to cool slightly.

Fill each clam shell (you will have 24) with a spoonful of mixture and top with a 1-inch piece of bacon. Set on a baking sheet and bake for 10 minutes, until the bacon browns.

Serve immediately with lemon wedges.

CHEF'S NOTES

- When purchasing **live clams** from your local fish market or supermarket, it is extremely important to inspect each clam to ensure that the shell is firmly closed. Even a slight opening in the shell means the clam is not safe to eat and should be discarded immediately.

- **Opening the clam shells** can be challenging, but your fishmonger will be able to halve the clams for you easily, thus eliminating a potentially time-consuming portion of this recipe.

See Season 4, Episode 401

VENISON TERRINE

SERVES 8 TO 12

Venison was a popular meat in colonial America as it was free for the hunting. There were many deer roaming the forests of the New World, but they quickly became over-hunted. By the early nineteenth century, venison was considered a delicacy.

In Europe, it was customary for royalty to lay claim to all the deer in the forests, which made venison out of reach for most. So terrine was then a dish that would have been served only to the upper echelon of society. During a visit to Paris, Benjamin Franklin fell in love with this dish; he would certainly have requested the recipe for his cook.

The recipe requires only a few steps but yields a tasty dish that would be as at home in an upscale Parisian bistro today as it was on Benjamin Franklin's dinner table. You can serve the terrine warm or cold, but I recommend serving it chilled with cranberry relish.

- 3 pounds bacon strips
- ½ cup chopped bacon
- 1 yellow onion, minced
- ½ cup chopped button mushrooms
- ½ cup chopped wild mushrooms
- ½ cup chopped fresh flat-leaf parsley
- 1 pound ground beef
- 2 pounds ground venison
- 2 eggs, lightly beaten
- 1 cup fresh bread crumbs
- ¼ cup cognac
- 1 teaspoon kosher salt
- 1 teaspoon freshly ground black pepper
- Cranberry relish, for serving

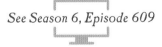

See Season 6, Episode 609

Preheat oven to 350°F.

Line the bacon strips in a 12½ by 4¼-inch terrine, overlapping the edges and allowing the excess to hang over the sides of the pan.

Fry the chopped bacon in a large skillet until crisp, 3 to 4 minutes. Add the onion, mushrooms, and parsley and cook until it becomes a semi-dry mixture, 5 to 8 minutes. Remove from the heat and allow to cool.

Once cooled, transfer to a large mixing bowl and add the ground beef and venison. Add the beaten eggs, bread crumbs, and cognac, mix well, and season with the salt and pepper.

Transfer the mixture to the bacon-lined loaf pan and pack it down. Fold the overhanging bacon on top of the mixture. Bake for 1½ hours. Cool on a rack.

When completely cool, cover and refrigerate for a few hours or overnight. Serve in thin slices with cranberry relish.

--- CHEF'S NOTES ---

❧ For those who may not have **venison** available to them, the terrine can be made with ground pork.

❧ The recipe calls for **wild mushrooms**, but a great alternative is the portobello mushroom. Not only are portobellos available in every supermarket, but they also deliver the rich flavor needed to complete the terrine.

❋ 2 ❋
SOUPS, STEWS, CHOWDERS, AND BISQUES

For All Tastes—Including Vegetarians

Most eighteenth-century meals were prepared over open hearths in large cast-iron pots hanging from sturdy wrought-iron cranes. This cooking technique, along with the necessity of using every bit of produce in the garden or root cellar, and every cut of meat in the larder, meant that soups, stews, and chowders were regular fare. While soups and stews may seem less exciting than other dishes at first glance, eighteenth-century Americans had a flare for incorporating new and exciting flavors into these hardworking, one-pot meals. They were eager to use foreign and imported food items, making for delicious recipes that can be tied back to the indelible influence of immigrants on American cuisine. A surprising variety of ingredients passed through the kitchen of an average family depending on the time of year—proving that seasonal eating and shopping was the norm hundreds of years before it became a restaurant trend.

Today, we have an easier life when it comes to access to food. We have the luxury of freezers and the convenience of supermarkets, but we still love soup. A bowl of soup (or stew or chowder) is welcoming, soothing, comforting, and satisfying. Soup is what we crave when we're feeling under the weather, or when we're housebound on a snowy, stormy day. A big pot of homemade soup is the perfect gift for new neighbors, just-home-from-the-hospital parents, or a friend in need of a pick-me-up.

Soup is easy on your wallet (you are often

using up odd bits of vegetables, or bones left over from a roast), and on your time: once the ingredients go into the pot, you can usually set a timer and walk away. And, if you like to bake, serving soup for dinner is the perfect way to show off a loaf of freshly baked bread. (See chapter 6, page 181, for a great collection of recipes for both yeasted and un-yeasted breads, biscuits, and rolls.) The beauty of the recipes in this chapter is that you can do much, if not all, of the prep in advance— handy for hosts and for busy families. Some recipes can be frozen, either as a finished dish or, more often, partially completed.

Cassoulet of Duck with White Beans and Root Vegetables

White Bean Soup

Beef Barley Soup

Chicken Noodle Soup

Eel and Mussel Bisque

Turkey and Rutabaga Stew

"Pease" Soup

Corn and Oyster Chowder

Cabbage Soup with Pork Dumplings

Crawfish Bisque

Lentil Stew with Rabbit

Philadelphia Pepper Pot

CASSOULET of DUCK with WHITE BEANS and ROOT VEGETABLES

SERVES 6 TO 8

WHEN GENERAL ROCHAMBEAU'S FIVE thousand French troops arrived in Newport, Rhode Island, to assist with the Revolution, the soldiers had to adjust their palate when faced with the cuisine of the New World. One food option, however, was quite familiar to the French: duck. Newport was teeming with ducks—but there was one catch: soldiers had to hunt the duck themselves—as opposed to visiting a butcher like back in Europe. This extra effort was rewarded with a little taste of home in a foreign land.

Soldiers often embarked on daily marches of twelve miles, so cassoulet would have been a perfect end to an exhausting day. The beans provide enough protein that this recipe could even be made without meat, although duck cassoulet was much preferred. Any meat can be substituted for the duck and will result in a hearty winter meal.

- 2 cups dried cannellini (navy) beans
- 1 (3 ½- to 5-pound) whole duck, cut into 16 pieces
- Kosher salt and freshly ground black pepper
- ¼ cup schmaltz (liquid fat, usually from chicken), use vegetable oil if not available
- 1 white onion, cut into medium dice
- 3 to 5 garlic cloves, chopped
- Slab bacon, cut into 1-inch lardons
- 2 quarts Chicken Stock (page 265 or store-bought)
- 1 medium carrot, peeled and cut into 1-inch cubes
- 1 medium rutabaga, peeled and cut into 1-inch cubes
- 8 medium white potatoes, cut into 1-inch cubes
- Roasted Pork Belly (prepared without the cabbage, page 146)
- Chopped fresh parsley, for garnish

To soak the beans: Place beans in a colander and rinse thoroughly with cold water to clean. Transfer to a large bowl and add water to cover by an inch or two. Cover and let stand at room temperature for at least 8 hours or overnight.

Drain again and thoroughly rinse the softened beans. Place beans in large saucepan, cover with water by 2 inches, and bring to a simmer. Cover and simmer for 1 hour. Drain water from beans.

To make the cassoulet: Season the duck with salt and pepper. Heat a large Dutch oven over medium-high heat and add the schmaltz (or oil). Add the duck pieces skin side down and sear until golden brown, about 5 minutes.

Turn the pieces over and brown the other side, then remove the duck from pot.

Add the onion, garlic, and bacon lardons to the Dutch oven and cook over medium-high heat until lightly browned. Add the beans, stock, carrot, and rutabaga and simmer for 25 to 30 minutes. Add the potatoes and simmer until the beans and potatoes are fork tender, 15 to 20 minutes. Add the duck and bring to a boil, then reduce the heat and simmer for 10 minutes, until the meat is pulling away from the bone.

Cut the pork belly into 2-inch chunks and add to the cassoulet right before serving for added texture. Garnish with parsley and serve.

CHEF'S NOTE

* Chefs were very frugal in the eighteenth century, making use of anything and everything available for cooking. The use of **schmaltz** reflects this practice. Schmaltz can come from chicken, pork— practically any animal fat; after roasting, the fat drippings were saved for future use.

See Season 9, Episode 911

WHITE BEAN SOUP

SERVES 8 TO 10

IN HIS GARDENS AT Monticello, Thomas Jefferson experimented with many different species of vegetables, herbs, and legumes. (He is reported to have had 350 distinct vegetable varieties!) One plant for which he was especially enthusiastic was the bean. He experimented with many varieties. Dried beans lasted forever, were easy to store, and provided an important source of nutrition during the winter months. While he enjoyed almost all, the cannellini bean (also known as white kidney bean) was among his favorites.

As a chef, it is easy for me to see why: white beans are a great source of protein, calcium, and a litany of other vitamins (most of which were unknown during Jefferson's lifetime), but most important, flavor. Subtle with nutty overtones and a hint of earthiness, white beans instantly add a different layer to a dish's flavor profile. They shine in this delicious soup.

- 1 pound dried cannellini (or navy) beans
- 2½ quarts Chicken Stock (page 265 or store-bought)
- ½ pound bacon, chopped
- 2 medium yellow onions, chopped
- 3 garlic cloves, chopped
- 2 cups chopped seeded fresh plum tomatoes (about 6 plum tomatoes)
- 1 tablespoon dried marjoram
- Kosher salt and freshly ground black pepper
- 3/4 cup finely chopped fresh parsley (about 1 bunch)

See Season 1, Episode 107

To soak the beans: Place the beans in a colander and rinse thoroughly with cold water to clean. Transfer to a large bowl and add water to cover by an inch or two. Cover and let stand at room temperature for at least 8 hours or overnight.

To make the soup: Drain again and thoroughly rinse the softened beans. Place the beans in a large stockpot, add the stock, and bring to a boil over high heat. Reduce the heat to low and simmer for about 1 hour, until the beans are soft.

Cook the bacon in a large skillet over medium heat. When crispy, 3 to 4 minutes, transfer the bacon to paper towels to drain. Do not discard the rendered fat in the skillet.

Add the onions and garlic to the fat and sauté for 5 minutes, until lightly browned. Add the tomatoes and sauté for 3 to 5 minutes more, until the tomatoes begin to dissolve.

Add the tomato mixture to the beans. Add the marjoram and cooked bacon and simmer the soup for about 10 minutes. Season with salt and pepper to taste. Just before serving, stir in the parsley.

CHEF'S NOTE

❧ For a spectacular **vegetarian version** of this soup, simply omit the bacon and substitute vegetable stock for the chicken stock.

BEEF BARLEY SOUP

SERVES 6

ON JUNE 18, 1795, Thomas Jefferson wrote "cut barley at Shadwell" in his *Farm Book*. As opposed to George Washington, who grew barley to feed the whiskey stills in his distillery, Jefferson seems to have grown barley for everyday meals. When settling back into Monticello in 1809, he wrote a letter to Gordon Trokes & Co., requesting ten pounds of pearl barley for the kitchens. Though colonial cooks used barley in many ways, it was most often served in soup; typically, barley soup included vegetables and mutton. Beef would have been substituted when mutton wasn't available.

- 1 tablespoon vegetable oil
- 1 pound beef chuck, trimmed and cut into 1-inch pieces
- 2 garlic cloves, finely chopped
- 2 large yellow onions, finely chopped
- 1 small celery root (celeriac), peeled and diced
- 2 large carrots, diced
- 2 quarts water
- 2 bay leaves
- 1 cup sliced button mushrooms
- ¾ cup pearl barley
- ¼ teaspoon dried thyme
- 2 tablespoons chopped fresh parsley
- Kosher salt and freshly ground black pepper

Heat the oil in a large stockpot or Dutch oven over medium heat. Add the beef and cook slowly until browned on all sides, 5 to 8 minutes. Add the garlic and cook over low heat until slightly soft, stirring to prevent burning. Add the onions and cook for 3 more minutes, until translucent but not browned. Add the celery root and carrots and cook until slightly soft, stirring often.

Pour in the water and add the bay leaves. Simmer over low heat for about 1 hour, or until the meat is tender. Stir in the mushrooms, barley, and thyme. Cook until the barley is tender, 15 to 20 minutes. Just before serving, remove the bay leaves, add the parsley, and season with salt and pepper to taste.

--- CHEF'S NOTE ---

- When I prepare this dish at home, I cook the **barley** on the side, adding it just before serving. This helps prevent the soup from becoming cloudy.

See Season 2, Episode 210

CHICKEN NOODLE SOUP

SERVES 6 TO 8

IN COLONIAL TIMES, CHICKENS were raised mainly for their eggs, which were prized for baking. Older chickens that no longer produced eggs were then used in stews and soups like this one. These chickens were fattier than younger hens, and colonial housewives used this to their advantage by rendering the fat to use as a flavorful alternative to butter or lard in other dishes. Adding egg noodles, a traditional German preparation, lent texture to the soup and served as a means of transforming it into a heartier meal that could feed an entire family.

- 1 medium onion, chopped
- 1 tablespoon unsalted butter
- 6 large stalks celery, chopped
- 3 large carrots, peeled and chopped
- 2 quarts Chicken Stock (page 265 or store-bought)
- 1 sprig fresh thyme
- 1 pound boneless chicken (white or dark meat), cooked and chopped
- 8 ounces egg noodles, cooked al dente and drained
- Kosher salt and freshly ground black pepper
- Chopped fresh parsley, for garnish

See Season 2, Episode 211

In a medium saucepan over medium heat, sauté the onion in the butter until softened and translucent, 3 to 5 minutes. Add the celery and carrots and sauté for 3 to 5 minutes more, until softened.

Stir in the stock and thyme and bring to a boil over high heat. Reduce the heat to low and simmer for about 30 minutes, until the stock is reduced by one-third. Lift out the thyme and discard, then add the chicken and egg noodles to the soup. Simmer until heated and season with salt and pepper.

Serve the soup in a tureen or in individual bowls garnished with parsley.

CHEF'S NOTE

- I recommend adding the **noodles** just before serving to prevent them from becoming overdone.

EEL AND MUSSEL BISQUE

SERVES 8

THIS CREAMY, LIGHTLY FLAVORED bisque is a classic European delight. The pieces of eel offer a delicate texture and the dish is finished with mussels in their shells. Eels were prevalent and easy to find in the colonial era, so they would have made the supper table regularly. Today, they are available in specialty shops and many Asian markets.

Mussels were a popular and readily available food for the colonists, but it was the Europeans' love of mother-of-pearl buttons that made the shells part of a multimillion-dollar business that continued well after the Revolutionary War.

- 9 tablespoons unsalted butter
- 2 tablespoons minced garlic
- 5 tablespoons diced shallots
- 2 pounds mussels (about 32 mussels) cleaned, debearded, and shells closed
- 4 cups dry white wine
- 2 eels (about 1 pound each), gutted and cleaned
- ¼ cup kosher salt
- Freshly ground black pepper
- 6 tablespoons cognac or brandy
- 2 cups sliced button mushrooms
- 1 leek, white part only, chopped
- 1 sprig fresh thyme
- 3 cups heavy cream
- 5 tablespoons all-purpose flour
- Chopped fresh parsley, for garnish

See Season 5, Episode 502

In a large stockpot with lid over medium heat, melt 2 tablespoons of the butter. Add 1 tablespoon of the garlic and 2 tablespoons of the shallots and cook until translucent. Add the mussels and 2 cups of the wine. Boil, covered, for about 5 minutes, or until all mussels have opened. Remove from heat and let rest with lid on.

Sprinkle the eels with the kosher salt and then wipe it all off to remove any slime. Cut the eels into 2-inch pieces. Discard the heads.

In a separate stockpot, melt 2 tablespoons of the remaining butter over medium heat. Add the remaining 1 tablespoon garlic and 3 tablespoons shallots and cook until translucent, 2 to 3 minutes. Add the eel pieces, turn the heat to high, and sauté for 5 to 8 minutes, until the eel begins to whiten. Season eel mixture with salt and pepper to taste.

Pour the cognac into a glass, then pour it into the eel mixture over high heat, and flambé: carefully hold a lighted long-stick match to the pan to ignite the alcohol. Once the fire has gone out, add just enough of the remaining 2 cups wine to cover the eel pieces. Add the mushrooms and leek and bring to a boil. Cook for 30 to 40 minutes on low heat, until the eel meat is cooked through and can easily be removed from bone. Add the thyme and cream and season with salt and pepper. Simmer for about 20 minutes, or until reduced slightly.

Remove the eel pot from the heat and strain the liquid into a separate, clean soup pot. Pick out the eel pieces, discard any bones, and set aside. Discard the vegetables and other solids. Strain the liquid from the mussels into the soup pot with the bisque and stir to combine. Set aside the mussels, still in their shells.

In a small bowl, combine the remaining 5 tablespoons butter (at room temperature) and

the flour to make a paste. Whisk a third of it into the bisque over low heat to thicken it. Continue to whisk more of the butter/flour mixture into the bisque until it reaches desired consistency, being careful not to make it too thick.

To serve, place the eel pieces and mussels in a soup tureen. Pour the bisque over the mussels and eel and garnish with fresh parsley.

CHEF'S NOTE

❦ Do not be intimidated by **eel**! The Asian supermarket or seafood shop where you purchase eel will have the meat completely cleaned and ready to cook.

TURKEY AND RUTABAGA STEW

SERVES 6 TO 8

THE TURKEY WAS NOTED in colonial writings as "undoubtedly one of the best gifts that the New World has made to the Old." Turkey was served throughout the colonies and enjoyed by all levels of society. They were so common in the Mid-Atlantic area during the eighteenth century that flocks numbering in the thousands could be found outside Philadelphia. These birds would often reach sizes of forty pounds or more.

This recipe is a rich and hearty dish inspired by General Anthony Wayne, in Paoli, who would have been blessed with an abundance of these birds. It is reasonable to believe that turkey would have been a staple in his troops' diet. General Wayne was also a man of means, and although he held the same frugal values that were common at the time, he also had the opportunity to finesse his meals a little more than the average man. The pork belly, a cut of meat that adds tremendous richness to the dish, is my tribute to his wealth.

- 2 tablespoons vegetable oil or schmaltz (see Chef's Note, page 38)
- 8 pounds skin-on turkey breast, cut into 2-inch cubes
- Kosher salt and freshly ground black pepper
- 1 large onion, cut into large dice
- 4 garlic cloves, coarsely chopped
- 2 quarts stock, broth, or water (chicken, turkey, vegetable stock all work well)
- 2 tablespoons fresh thyme leaves
- 12 medium turnips, peeled and cut into ½-inch cubes
- 2 medium rutabagas, peeled and cut into ¼-inch-thick slices
- Roasted Pork Belly (prepared without the cabbage, page 146)

Preheat oven to 350°F.

In a Dutch oven or large ovenproof stockpot, heat the oil (or schmaltz) over medium-high heat. Season the turkey with salt and pepper. Cook the turkey cubes in the oil, skin side down, for about 10 minutes per side, until the turkey is caramelized. Add the onion and garlic and cook until the onion is translucent and starting to brown at the edges, about 4 minutes. Add half of the stock (1 quart) and the thyme and bring to a simmer. Cover the pot, transfer to the oven, and bake for 1 hour.

Add the remaining stock, turnips, and rutabaga. Continue to bake until the vegetables are tender, approximately 15 minutes.

Cut the pork belly into 3- to 3½-inch chunks, using the cuts in the skin as guides. Fold the pork belly into the stew. Adjust seasoning with salt and pepper as desired and serve.

CHEF'S NOTE

❧ The **turnip** adds a distinct flavor and also lends the same thickening properties as flour.

See Season 9, Episode 901

"PEASE" SOUP

SERVES 10 TO 12

THE SPLIT PEA IS actually a field pea, a variety of yellow or green pea grown specifically for drying. Dried peas and beans were an important staple for the colonists, because they could be stored easily and would last indefinitely. They also traveled well, making them a common item for cooking on the wagon trails.

Using the peas to make soup was common in colonial times. Cookbooks of the era refer to these as white peas, presumably for the light color they develop when dried. Martha Washington used "white pease" in her recipe "To Make Pease Porrage of Old Peas," which includes coriander and mint, thought to guard against indigestion and "windiness."

- 1 pound dried split peas
- 4 tablespoons unsalted butter
- ½ pound lean bacon, finely chopped
- 1 large white onion, chopped
- 2 garlic cloves, chopped
- 3 quarts Chicken Stock (page 265 or store-bought)
- Kosher salt and freshly ground black pepper

See Season 6, Episode 603

Place the split peas in a colander and rinse thoroughly with cold water to clean. Transfer to a large bowl and cover with water. Let stand at room temperature for at least 8 hours or overnight (preferred). Drain, rinse, and set aside.

Melt the butter in a large stockpot over medium heat. Add the bacon and sauté for 3 minutes. Add the onion and garlic and sauté until golden brown. Add the split peas and stock and bring to a boil over high heat. Season with salt and pepper to taste. Reduce the heat to medium and cook for about 1½ hours, until the split peas have dissolved. Transfer to a soup tureen, or ladle directly into bowls, and serve.

CHEF'S NOTES

- For a **vegetarian version** of this soup, omit the bacon and substitute vegetable stock for the chicken stock.
- To take this recipe over the top, I like to garnish it with **Herb Croutons** (page 251).

CORN AND OYSTER CHOWDER

SERVES 8 TO 10

THIS HEARTY CHOWDER IS an excellent example of Old and New World cuisine combining to create something uniquely American. Oysters are available in the wild across the globe and have been prepared by humans for millennia; evidence of oyster consumption has been found in caves occupied by some of the earliest people. Corn, on the opposite extreme, is a "new" ingredient, in the global sense. While Native Americans have used corn for a variety of dishes for centuries, the rest of the world was unaware of its many uses until European contact.

The combination of corn and oyster is a delightful one; the soft briny flavor of the oyster pairs perfectly with the subtle sweetness of corn.

- 2 tablespoons unsalted butter
- 1 cup chopped carrots (2 to 3 carrots)
- 1 cup chopped celery (3 to 4 stalks)
- 1 cup chopped onion (1 medium-large onion)
- 1 quart Vegetable Stock (page 268 or store-bought)
- 1 tablespoon chopped shallot
- 1 tablespoon chopped fresh basil
- 1 teaspoon chopped fresh thyme
- 1 teaspoon sweet paprika
- 3 garlic cloves, chopped
- 3 large russet potatoes (about 1 pound), peeled and diced
- 10 ears fresh white corn, kernels cut from cobs
- 2 cups heavy cream

- 1 pint shucked oysters (approximately 20 oysters)
- ¼ cup cornstarch
- ¼ cup dry white wine, such as Sauvignon Blanc
- Chopped fresh chives or scallions, for garnish

Melt the butter in a medium stockpot over medium heat. Add the carrots, celery, and onion and sauté until the onions are translucent, 3 to 4 minutes. Add the stock, shallot, basil, thyme, paprika, and garlic and bring to a boil. Stir in the potatoes and corn kernels and bring back to a boil. Stir in the cream. Add the oysters and reduce the heat. Simmer, stirring occasionally, until the vegetables are tender and the soup is heated through, about 5 minutes. *Do not allow the soup to boil or the oysters will be overdone and chewy!*

In a small bowl, combine the cornstarch and wine; mix until velvety smooth. Add some of the hot soup to the cornstarch mixture and stir until the mixture is thin. Gently stir the cornstarch mixture back into the soup. Cook for 3 to 5 minutes, or until desired thickness is achieved. Serve garnished with chives (or scallions).

CHEF'S NOTES

- This recipe is very versatile. Try substituting 1 pint lump **crabmeat or 20 small shrimp** for the oysters—both make for excellent flavor profiles.

- As with most cream-based soups, you can **substitute half-and-half** for the cream without giving up too much flavor or consistency.

See Season 8, Episode 807

CABBAGE SOUP WITH PORK DUMPLINGS

SERVES 6 TO 8

Savoy cabbage is thought to have originated in the Netherlands, but by the eighteenth century cultivation of this varietal had spread across Europe. It was popular in many countries but none more so than Germany, where it is used for sauerkraut, roulades, and other traditional German dishes. It lends a bit of sweetness and texture to this interesting soup, while the pork dumplings add a unique depth of flavor.

- ¼ cup pork schmaltz (see Chef's Notes, page 38) or vegetable oil
- 1 onion, cut into 1-inch cubes
- 3 garlic cloves, coarsely chopped
- 1 pound bacon, chopped
- 2 pounds ground pork
- 1 cup fresh bread crumbs
- 3 eggs
- ¼ cup chopped fresh chives
- 3 cups Chicken Stock (page 265 or store-bought)
- Kosher salt and freshly ground black pepper
- 2 heads savoy cabbage, cored and cut into 2-inch flags (squares)
- 6 Irish white potatoes (or Yukon Gold), cut into 8 pieces each
- 2 tablespoons chopped fresh parsley

Set a large frying pan over medium heat and add the oil (or schmaltz), onion, garlic, and bacon. Cook lightly until the onion is translucent, 3 to 4 minutes, and remove from heat.

In a large bowl, mix together the ground pork, bread crumbs, eggs, and chives. Mix with hands to combine thoroughly. Add the onion mixture and combine well. Form the mixture into dumplings (meatballs), using a heaping teaspoon for each and making them all about the same size.

In a large stockpot, bring the stock to a boil, then reduce to a strong simmer over medium heat. Using a slotted spoon, add the dumplings to the stock and cook at a simmer until cooked through, about 5 minutes, when the dumplings begin floating. Season with salt and pepper and add the cabbage and potatoes. Continue to cook at a simmer until the cabbage is wilted and potatoes are fork tender, about 10 minutes. Add the parsley and serve.

CHEF'S NOTES

- I recommend savoy **cabbage** for this soup, but you can use whichever cabbage you find available.
- This ode to the Irish in America is a wonderful one-pot meal served with **Irish Soda Bread** (page 186).

See Season 6, Episode 605

CRAWFISH BISQUE

SERVES 6 TO 8

WHEN THINKING OF CRAWFISH, most people's thoughts automatically go to the Cajun cuisine of the Gulf Coast. So it may come as a surprise that these tiny crustaceans were readily available in streams and rivers all over the colonies. From the northern reaches of New England to the swamps of the Deep South, crawfish (also known then as river shrimp) were eaten by many. Because they lived in shallow water, crawfish were easily gathered by men, women, and children alike—all of which made crawfish a common feature on the dinner table in the eighteenth century.

This recipe is a bisque made in the European tradition, with the cognac, cream, and subtle herbs complementing the flavor of the crawfish.

- ¾ cup (1½ sticks) unsalted butter
- 2 pounds whole crawfish (or 1 pound lobster tail meat if whole crawfish are not available)
- ½ cup cognac
- 2 medium-large shallots, coarsely chopped
- 3 bunches scallions (white parts only), chopped
- ½ teaspoon freshly ground black pepper
- 3 bay leaves
- ¼ cup white wine
- 8 to 10 sprigs fresh thyme
- 1 cup whole milk
- ¼ cup all-purpose flour
- ¼ cup heavy cream
- Kosher salt and freshly ground black pepper
- Chopped fresh parsley (for garnish)

In a large stockpot, melt 8 tablespoons (1 stick) of the butter over medium-high heat. Add the crawfish and cognac and cook for 5 minutes. Strain the liquid into a bowl and return to stockpot. Set aside the crawfish.

Add the shallots, scallions, pepper, and bay leaves to the stockpot. Bring to a boil and then reduce heat to a simmer. Add the wine and half of the thyme sprigs (whole, including stems). Stir and let simmer for 5 minutes over low heat. Add the milk and allow to simmer for another 30 to 45 minutes, allowing flavors to marry.

In a small bowl, combine the remaining 4 tablespoons butter (softened) with the flour until well mixed (this is the *beurre manié*). Add the *beurre manié* to the bisque in small batches, whisking well after each addition, until thickened to a gravy-like consistency. Add the remaining thyme (leaves only, about 1 tablespoon). Return the crawfish to the pot, add the cream, and bring to barely a simmer. Season to taste with salt and pepper, garnish with parsley, and serve.

CHEF'S NOTE

❦ If the **consistency** of the bisque is too thick, add more cream; if it is not thick enough, whisk in more *beurre manié*.

See Season 7, Episode 701

LENTIL STEW WITH RABBIT

SERVES 4

EARLY GERMAN SETTLERS PREPARED lentils frequently—and to this day lentil soup is a common item on Amish and Pennsylvania Dutch menus. Adding a bit of chopped sausage or virtually any kind of smoked cut of pork boosts the flavor of this hearty stew.

- 3 cups yellow lentils
- 1 whole rabbit, skinned and cleaned
- Kosher salt and freshly ground black pepper
- ½ cup schmaltz (see Chef's Notes, page 38), or lard (or vegetable oil)
- 4 ounces slab bacon, chopped
- ½ cup red wine
- Up to 1 quart Beef Stock (page 264 or store-bought)
- 1 medium white onion, chopped
- 1 carrot, cut into medium dice
- 6 red bliss potatoes, cut into medium dice
- 1 garlic clove, minced
- 2 bay leaves
- 1 tablespoon dried thyme

Place the lentils in a colander and rinse thoroughly with cold water to clean. Transfer to a large bowl, cover with water, cover, and let stand at room temperature for at least 8 hours or overnight (preferred). Drain, rinse, and set aside.

Chop the rabbit, with the bones, into 16 small pieces. Season with salt and pepper.

Heat a Dutch oven over medium-high heat. Add the schmaltz (or lard or oil), then the rabbit and bacon. When the bacon begins to render its fat, in 2 to 3 minutes, add the wine and deglaze the pot, stirring with a wooden spoon to loosen any brown bits on the bottom. Add 1 cup of the beef stock, the onion, carrot, potatoes, garlic, bay leaves, and thyme. Bring to a boil and then reduce to a simmer. Add the lentils and enough of the remaining beef stock to come just below the vegetable/lentil level. Continue to cook until the lentils begin to break apart and dissolve, 1 to 1½ hours. Remove and discard the bay leaves. Check seasoning and adjust with salt and pepper as needed before serving.

CHEF'S NOTES

- This recipe easily lends itself to be made with other meats, such as a whole 3-pound **chicken** cut into 8 or 10 pieces.
- For a **vegetarian** option, omit the bacon and rabbit, and use vegetable oil and vegetable stock.

See Season 7, Episode 708

PHILADELPHIA PEPPER POT

SERVES 6

In Season 8 of *A Taste of History*, I had the pleasure of featuring the story of the Mummers Parade, a tradition in Philadelphia that goes back to the seventeenth century. The Mummers still draw crowds of thousands every New Year's morning for their famous folk celebration.

Upon first entering the Mummers Museum in South Philadelphia, your eyes are immediately drawn to the bold letters painted across the wall—a poem that was chanted door-to-door during the early days of the Mummers:

> *Here we stand before your door,*
> *As we stood the year before;*
> *Give us whisky, give us gin,*
> *Open the door and let us in.*
> *Or give us something nice and hot*
> *Like a steaming hot bowl of pepperpot!*

There are a couple of variations to this spicy soup, including a West Indies variation that I serve at City Tavern. This recipe, however, is the true Philadelphia Pepper Pot—the same soup that would have been enjoyed in the frigid air of January 1 by the elaborately costumed Mummers.

- 1½ pounds cleaned honeycomb tripe (or salt-cured pork shoulder)
- 3 tablespoons unsalted butter
- 2 onions, chopped
- 2 carrots, diced
- 2 stalks celery, diced
- 2 garlic cloves, sliced
- 1 tablespoon fresh thyme leaves
- 3 sprigs of fresh rosemary
- 3 bay leaves
- 3 cloves
- 3 to 5 tablespoons black peppercorns, crushed
- Cayenne pepper, to taste
- 2 quarts Beef Stock (page 264)

Rinse the tripe (or pork) in cold water, place in a large pan, cover with water, and simmer for 20 minutes. Drain and allow it to cool. Cut into bite-size cubes.

Melt the butter in a Dutch oven over medium-high heat. Add the onions, carrots, celery, and garlic and sauté until just soft, about 3 minutes. Add the cooked tripe (or pork), thyme, rosemary, bay leaves, cloves, peppercorns, cayenne, and stock to the pot. Add enough water to cover all ingredients and bring to a simmer. Skim off any foam that floats to the top, and continue to simmer for 1½ to 2 hours. Remove rosemary sprigs and bay leaf. Serve immediately.

See Season 8, Episode 810

CHEF'S NOTES

❧ This soup pairs perfectly with a thick slice of **Cornbread** (page 203).

❧ **Tripe**, the honeycombed lining of a cow's stomach, has a long history of use in Spain, France, and Italy. Never willing to waste a single part of an animal, colonials consumed tripe in soups and stews, slow cooked to a buttery tenderness.

❋ 3 ❋
SALADS

Salads of Greens, Vegetables, Fruits, and Legumes

In colonial America, vegetables were grown in abundance and comprised a significant part of colonists' diets but, interestingly, they were rarely eaten raw—including leafy greens. That custom had a number of factors behind it: Cooking fresh vegetables interrupted their ability to spoil, which provided a longer window to eat them. Vegetables were also raised with an eye toward what would store well in a root cellar. The ones that met that criterion tended to be hard-fleshed; cooking tenderized them, released and enhanced their flavor, and allowed any blemishes to go unnoticed. When only a few vegetables were available to feed a whole family, a cooked preparation (perhaps with the addition of spices, herbs, or bits of meat) meant the cook could pull off a bit of a culinary magic trick—turning a few odds and ends into a full meal. In addition, historians have pointed out that food that is easy to chew was a boon to those missing a few teeth—a not uncommon condition for the colonists.

All this is to say that fresh salads, as we think of them today, were not part of eighteenth-century cuisine. My research, however, has unearthed a tasty collection of dishes the colonists did enjoy that qualify as salads on the twenty-first-century table. If you are a member of a CSA or someone who frequents farmers' markets, I hope you'll enjoy the new ideas you'll find here for seasonal, vegetable-forward dishes that withstand the test of time.

Roasted Red and Golden Beet Salad

Tripe with Bitter Melon

Black Forest Mâche Salad

Marinated Leeks

Fennel Salad with Bacon Vinaigrette

Mom's Potato Salad

Hot and Spicy Cabbage Slaw

French Lentil Salad

ROASTED RED AND GOLDEN BEET SALAD

SERVES 6

COLONIAL CHEFS SHOULD HAVE considered beets the perfect vegetable—they stored well over the winter and were extremely versatile in soups, salads, and relishes. Even so, Mary Randolph noted in *The Virginia Housewife* that red beets "are not so much used as they deserve to be." She seems to have made good use of them, however, noting after one recipe for boiling beets that they are "an excellent garnish, and easily converted into a very cheap and pleasant pickle."

This recipe was inspired by Mary Randolph's love of beets, and I believe that she would be proud of this dish. While she suggested boiling, I have found that roasting provides the best results.

- 1 pound fresh red beets, stems trimmed ½ inch from the beets

- 1 pound fresh golden beets, stems trimmed ½ inch from the beets

- 2 eggs

- 1 cup olive oil

- ¼ cup red wine vinegar

- Juice of ½ lemon (1 generous tablespoon)

- 1 tablespoon Dijon mustard

- ½ cup finely chopped onion (approximately 1 small onion)

- 1 tablespoon chopped fresh parsley

- ½ teaspoon red pepper flakes

- Kosher salt and freshly ground black pepper

- ½ cup roughly chopped walnuts

- Romaine lettuce leaves, for serving (optional)

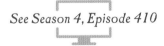

See Season 4, Episode 410

Preheat oven to 350°F.

Line two shallow baking dishes with foil. Add the red beets to one dish and the golden beets to the other. Roast until they can be pierced, with slight resistance, by a sharp knife, 30 to 45 minutes (the smaller golden beets will cook more quickly). Let cool slightly. When cool enough to handle, use a small paring knife to remove the beet skins. Cut the beets into 1-inch cubes and set aside.

Hard-boil the eggs: Place the eggs in a small saucepan, cover with cold water, and set over high heat. As soon as the water reaches a boil, turn off the heat, cover the pan with a tight-fitting lid, and let sit for 9 minutes. Drain and then rinse under cold running water until the shells are cool enough to handle. Remove the shells, chop the eggs into small dice, and set aside.

In a medium mixing bowl, whisk together the oil, vinegar, lemon juice, mustard, onion, parsley, and red pepper flakes. Season with salt and pepper to taste. Using a wooden spoon, gently stir in the beets, chopped eggs, and walnuts. Cover the bowl with plastic wrap and refrigerate for about 2 hours, until the salad is marinated and thoroughly chilled. Adjust seasoning to taste and serve as is, or on one or two tender inner leaves of romaine lettuce.

CHEF'S NOTES

❧ For an enhanced flavor, toast the **walnuts** to release their oils.

❧ The main caveat for **beet** preparation: I recommend not boiling them as it can have an adverse effect on their color, texture, and flavor.

TRIPE WITH BITTER MELON

SERVES 4 TO 6

TRIPE MAY NOT BE as popular in America as it once was, but early Americans would not waste any part of the animal, including the stomach. Now more common in Asian and Caribbean recipes, this underappreciated ingredient is one I hope you'll try. Should your local butcher not carry it, you will find tripe widely available in Asian supermarkets.

I first tasted this salad in China. The combination of tripe and melon is incredible. Bitter melon is related to watermelon and cantaloupe, but in appearance it is similar to a cucumber. The name is misleading; the melon *is* bitter—but in a wonderful way. It provides great contrast in many dishes, especially true in this recipe.

- 6 tablespoons vegetable oil
- 1 (1-inch) piece fresh ginger, peeled and sliced in half lengthwise
- 6 to 8 garlic cloves, peeled
- 2 to 4 whole fresh star anise pods
- 2 to 3 tablespoons Szechuan peppercorns
- 1 teaspoon black peppercorns
- 2 cinnamon sticks
- 6 bay leaves
- Orange peel from 1 orange, pith removed
- 6 cups water
- ¼ cup sherry
- ⅓ cup soy sauce
- 1 teaspoon salt
- 8 ounces cleaned honeycomb tripe
- 1 bitter melon
- 1 red bell pepper, julienned
- 1 to 2 teaspoons sesame oil
- ½ teaspoon Szechuan powder
- White pepper
- Spicy oil or hot sauce, to taste

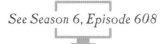

See Season 6, Episode 608

Heat 3 to 4 tablespoons of the oil in a large frying pan (or wok, if available) over medium-high heat. Add the ginger, garlic, anise, Szechuan peppercorns, black peppercorns, cinnamon sticks, bay leaves, and orange peel. Cook until the oils begin to release, about 1 minute. Add 4 cups water, the sherry, soy sauce, and salt and bring to a boil. Add the tripe and boil for 45 minutes, until tender. Set aside.

Meanwhile, wash the bitter melon and remove the ends. Split in half lengthwise, remove core, and slice into ⅛-inch crescent slices. In a medium saucepan, combine 2 cups water and the remaining 2 to 3 tablespoons oil and bring to a gentle boil. Add the bitter melon slices and blanch for about 1 minute. Drain and transfer the melon to a mixing bowl. Add the bell pepper.

Remove the cooked tripe from the wok and slice into thin (about ¼-inch) strips. Add to the melon and bell pepper, then toss together with the sesame oil, Szechuan powder, white pepper, and your favorite spicy oil or hot sauce.

Plate and serve at room temperature.

CHEF'S NOTE

- This dish makes a great salad when served over a small bed of **greens.**

BLACK FOREST MÂCHE SALAD

SERVES 4 TO 6

THE FRENCH HAVE ENJOYED mâche, a sweet, nutty deep-colored salad green, since the seventeenth century, and today it is a favorite of most Europeans. As with many vegetables in eighteenth-century America, mâche was widely known because of the European influences in the colonies. Thomas Jefferson is reported to have grown mâche in his gardens at Monticello. The small leaves are not the only distinction that sets this leafy green apart from other lettuces; the flavor is unique, as is its soft texture.

- 4 cups mâche, washed and dried
- 4 hard-boiled eggs (see page 64), peeled and chopped
- 8 ounces bacon, cut into ½-inch pieces
- 2 tablespoons red wine vinegar
- ¼ cup hazelnuts, chopped coarsely and toasted

See Season 6, Episode 611

Place the mâche in a large bowl and top with the hard-boiled eggs.

In a large frying pan over medium heat, cook the bacon until crisp, 3 or 4 minutes. Remove the pan from heat and add the vinegar to the pan; stir to combine.

Pour the bacon vinaigrette onto the mâche and top with hazelnuts. Serve immediately.

CHEF'S NOTE

- You should always **wash any produce** prior to preparing in a recipe, but pay extra close attention to mâche. If purchased at a farmers' market, a more intense washing may be needed, due to the unique shape.

MARINATED LEEKS

SERVES 6

IN THE EIGHTEENTH CENTURY, chefs were always in desperate search for color—especially in the winter when relying heavily on a root cellar for daily meals. Leeks were highly valued for their flavor and versatility, as well as for their vibrant green color. They could (and still can) be left frozen in the field until ready to cook.

This simple dish is very French in that it uses few ingredients and a classic cooking technique, resulting in a beautiful dish that seems greater than the sum of its parts.

- 1½ pounds leeks, top third (dark green) removed
- 1 hard-boiled egg (see page 64), peeled and chopped
- ½ red onion, finely chopped
- 1 tablespoon fine capers, drained
- ½ cup olive oil
- 2 tablespoons rice vinegar
- Pinch of fresh thyme
- Pinch of chopped fresh parsley
- Kosher salt and freshly ground white pepper

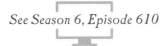

See Season 6, Episode 610

Slice the leeks almost in half lengthwise, leaving an inch at the base intact, and wash them well in cold water to remove any grit. Then, tie the individual leeks with cooking twine to prevent them from falling apart.

In a large saucepan, bring 2 quarts of lightly salted water to a boil over high heat. Add the leeks and cook until just tender, 5 to 6 minutes. Drain and set leeks aside to cool.

In a medium mixing bowl, whisk together the egg, onion, capers, olive oil, vinegar, thyme, and parsley. Add salt and pepper to taste. Place the leeks on a serving platter, pour the vinaigrette evenly over the leeks, and serve.

CHEF'S NOTE

- These leeks will work nicely as both a salad or as an **appetizer.**

FENNEL SALAD WITH BACON VINAIGRETTE

SERVES 8

FENNEL IS USED OFTEN in Middle Eastern and Central Asian cuisine, but it was the German and Italian immigrants who brought it to their New World gardens and dinner tables. It was so widely cultivated in America during the colonial time that it spread into the wild; now, in certain parts of America, it is considered invasive! While it may be unwelcomed by farmers who were not expecting it in their fields, this member of the carrot family provides great complexity to even the simplest dish. It is a hardy perennial with feathery leaves, beautiful yellow flowers, and strong aromatic qualities. The flavor is similar to anise but more delicate, which makes it suitable for a wide range of cuisines. Thomas Jefferson was a notable fan of fennel; he was introduced to the ingredient during his time in France and brought fennel back to plant in his personal gardens at Monticello.

- 6 slices lean bacon, cut into thin strips
- ¼ cup balsamic vinegar
- 2 garlic cloves, chopped
- ½ red onion, finely sliced
- 2½ pounds fresh fennel, bulb only, cored and finely sliced
- Herb Croutons (page 251)
- Kosher salt and freshly ground black pepper

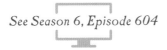

See Season 6, Episode 604

In a large frying pan over medium heat, cook the bacon until crisp, 3 or 4 minutes. Transfer the bacon to a paper towel–lined plate and set aside. Reserve the drippings in the pan.

In a small bowl, whisk together the balsamic vinegar, garlic, and red onion. Add a tablespoon of the bacon drippings and continue to whisk until combined.

To serve, place the fennel and croutons in a large salad bowl and toss. Drizzle the vinaigrette over the salad and toss again lightly. Add the crisp bacon strips and toss again. Season to taste with salt and pepper.

MOM'S POTATO SALAD

SERVES 6

POTATO SALAD [CALLED *KARTOFFELSALAT*] is a popular German dish. For this recipe, I traveled to Frankfurt, Germany, to spend time with my mother in the kitchen and watch her create our family's version. It is a recipe that goes back at least five generations, and I am pleased to present you with the recipe, which has been, until now, a Staib family secret.

With the large German population in eighteenth-century America, and the popularity of potatoes, this dish (or one close to it) would likely have been enjoyed by the colonists.

- 12 medium Yukon Gold potatoes
- 1 large yellow onion, finely chopped
- ¼ cup red wine vinegar
- ¼ cup vegetable oil
- 1½ to 2 cups Beef Stock (page 264 or store-bought)
- Kosher salt and freshly ground white pepper
- 2 hard-boiled eggs (see page 64), peeled and cut into eighths
- Chopped fresh chives, for garnish

Place the potatoes in a large saucepan or stockpot with enough salted water to cover. Bring to a boil over high heat and cook until the potatoes are just tender, 15 to 20 minutes (depending on size of potato). Drain the potatoes in a colander. When cool enough to handle, peel and cut into ¼-inch-thick slices.

In a medium bowl, combine the potatoes and onion. Add the vinegar and oil, tossing gently to coat. Pour in the stock, a little at a time, mixing gently until it is absorbed (the salad should be moist, but not drenched). Season with salt and white pepper.

Garnish with hard-boiled eggs and chives and serve while the potatoes are still slightly warm, or at room temperature (not chilled).

CHEF'S NOTES

- My mom always made her own **beef stock,** but you certainly do not have to. Any store-bought broth or stock will work perfectly fine for this dish.

- I strongly urge you to use **Yukon Gold potatoes** for this recipe. The golden yellow color and the flavor of this potato are perfectly suited for this style of potato salad. When making this, or any other potato salad, cook the potatoes in their skins and then peel them; this prevents them from becoming waterlogged.

See Season 6, Episode 611

HOT AND SPICY CABBAGE SLAW

 SERVES 8

COLONIAL CULTIVATORS TOOK FULL advantage of every growing window available to them. Cabbage can have two successful crops a year—both spring and fall—so it was a staple in the colonial diet. Back then, this dish would have been eaten when cabbage was freshly picked. But it holds up extremely well in a root cellar and would, therefore, have made regular appearances on dinner tables throughout the fall, and it could be prepared with preserved cabbage later on in the winter.

The spice element may remind you of kimchi, but this is a recipe that would have been enjoyed in Philadelphia during the eighteenth century.

- 1 medium savoy cabbage (2 to 2½ pounds), shredded very fine
- 2 scallions, finely chopped
- 1 tablespoon sugar
- 1 tablespoon chopped fresh parsley
- 1 teaspoon crushed red pepper flakes
- 1 tablespoon kosher salt
- ½ teaspoon freshly ground black pepper
- 4 ounces bacon, chopped
- ¼ cup red wine vinegar
- ¼ cup olive oil

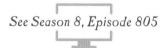

See Season 8, Episode 805

In a large bowl, thoroughly combine the cabbage, scallions, sugar, parsley, pepper flakes, salt, and black pepper.

In a large frying pan over medium heat, cook the bacon until crisp, 3 or 4 minutes. Add the vinegar and olive oil, stir with a wooden spoon, and pour over the cabbage mixture. Immediately cover the bowl with plastic wrap or a pot lid and let the salad sit for 10 to 15 minutes, steaming the cabbage to your desired texture. Adjust seasoning of salt and pepper and serve.

—— CHEF'S NOTE ——

- While my personal favorite **cabbage** for this recipe is savoy, any cabbage that you may happen to have will work nicely.

FRENCH LENTIL SALAD

SERVES 8

THIS SOPHISTICATED FRENCH SALAD might have been served at City Tavern in the eighteenth century—restaurant chefs of the era strove to incorporate French and European dishes into colonial menus, using the ingredients at hand (including dried beans and lentils) with great creativity.

Lentils are one of the most versatile ingredients, and recipes utilizing the legume range from rustic fare to elegant cuisine. While there are several styles of lentils, smaller, darker French lentils were the most highly prized during the eighteenth century and are, arguably, even today.

FOR THE SALAD

- 4 cups dried French lentils
- 2 carrots, peeled and julienned
- 1 medium yellow onion, chopped
- 2 large garlic cloves, chopped
- 1 bay leaf
- 3 sprigs fresh thyme
- 1 teaspoon kosher salt
- ½ teaspoon freshly ground black pepper

FOR THE DRESSING

- 1 red onion, finely chopped
- ½ cup olive oil
- ¼ cup red wine vinegar
- 1 bunch fresh chives, chopped (about 6 tablespoons)
- 2 tablespoons Dijon mustard
- 3 garlic cloves, chopped
- 1 teaspoon kosher salt
- ½ teaspoon freshly ground black pepper

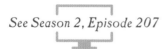

See Season 2, Episode 207

Make the salad: In a large saucepan, combine the lentils, carrots, onion, garlic, bay leaf, thyme, salt, and pepper. Add enough water to cover and bring just to a boil over high heat. Immediately reduce the heat to low, cover the pan, and cook at a simmer until the lentils are tender, but not overcooked; check after 20 minutes. Check frequently for doneness during cooking as overcooking will break down the lentils and change the texture of the dish. Drain the lentil mixture in a colander and transfer to a large bowl. Remove and discard the thyme sprigs and bay leaf. Cover the lentils and refrigerate for 1 hour, until thoroughly chilled.

Make the dressing: Combine the red onion, olive oil, vinegar, chives, mustard, garlic, salt, and pepper in a large bowl.

Add the lentil mixture to the dressing and mix gently to coat. Season with additional salt and pepper to taste. Let stand at room temperature for about 30 minutes to allow the flavors to develop. Give the lentils a final toss before serving.

CHEF'S NOTES

- I have served this dish many times as a main course by simply adding my favorite **bacon or sausage.**
- Although there is a wide variety of lentils at the market, only **French lentils** should be used in this recipe.

✳ 4 ✳

MAIN DISHES

Roasts, Chops, Seafood, Savory Pies, and Casseroles

In eighteenth-century America, dinners were most often what we today call one-dish meals, which is to say that almost the entire meal would be cooked in one pot, roasting pan, or casserole dish. Many of the recipes in this chapter largely fit that description, making for dinners that work well for twenty-first-century families. This style of cooking is popular again today—simplifying dinnertime when both parents work or the children's extracurricular activities keep everyone playing beat-the-clock. One-dish meals are also perfect for hosts who want to spend more time with dinner guests and less time facing the stove. Whether it's Benjamin Franklin's Stuffed Lobster for a special dinner or Thomas Jefferson's Cabbage Pudding for a casual family dinner, there are recipes here for every occasion.

In this chapter, you'll find meat and seafood dishes that present a wonderfully diverse selection of choices to suit your palate, pocketbook, and the time of year. International influences made a mark on eighteenth-century American cooking, so many main dishes—including curries, wine sauces, citrus marinades, fiery hot peppers, spice rubs, and cream sauces—that originated far from the shores of colonial America were readily adopted. In the recipes that call for ingredients that might be difficult to find today, I've listed alternatives that make cooking these historical feasts doable for home cooks. If you own a cast-iron Dutch oven, you can cook in virtually the same manner as the colonists—but on your modern cooktop rather than over a wood-burning fire on an open hearth.

Cabbage Pudding (Stuffed Cabbage)

Bouilli (Boiled Beef)

Chicken Fricassee

West Indies Curried Lamb

Shrimp in Saffron Cream

Cornmeal-Fried Catfish

Baked Stuffed Sturgeon

Curried Shrimp and Tofu

Veal Kidney Dijonnaise

Roasted Pheasant

Curried Chicken

Tripe à la Mode

New England Boiled Dinner

Guyanese Duck Curry

Coq au Vin Rouge

Beef Royale

Veal Tongue Fricassee

Shrimp and Rutabaga Fricassee

Stuffed Lobster

Calf Livers in Calvados

Fried Sweetbreads

Sauerbraten

Fried Soft-Shell Crabs

Fried Rabbit

Braised Lamb Shanks

Braised Bluefish

Elk Stew

Roasted Pork Belly with Cabbage

Lavender Duck Breast

Snapper Doré

Nicaraguan Beef Tongue

CABBAGE PUDDING (STUFFED CABBAGE)

THE NAME *PUDDING* MAY bring to mind a dessert, but in the eighteenth century puddings were similar to sausage—a variety of meats or other ingredients cooked in cloth and then sliced. This is one of the recipes copied out by Jefferson himself, originally titled "A Cabbage Pudding" and inspired by a recipe in Hannah Glasse's 1745 cookbook.

Cooked whole and wrapped in a cloth, this stuffed cabbage is a good example of the common and popular savory boiled puddings of the era. I have adapted Jefferson's recipe with details from Mary Randolph's rendition, mixing some of the heart of the cabbage with the stuffing and serving it "whole with a little melted butter in the dish." Since Jefferson only listed "sweet herbs," I've chosen the herbs usually used with beef during that time. Originally, the beef was finely chopped by hand, but you can use ground beef.

- 1 large green cabbage (about 2 pounds)
- 1 pound ground beef (preferably 80/20 ration of lean/fat)
- 1 small white onion, minced
- 1 tablespoon chopped fresh parsley, plus additional for garnish
- 1 tablespoon chopped fresh herbs, such as thyme, marjoram, or summer savory (or 2 teaspoons dried herbs)
- ½ cup fresh bread crumbs
- 3 eggs
- ½ teaspoon kosher salt
- ¼ teaspoon freshly ground black pepper
- 4 tablespoons unsalted butter, melted

See Season 1, Episode 105

Bring a large stockpot of salted water to a boil over high heat. The pot should be deep enough to submerge the cabbage completely.

Remove any blemished outer leaves of cabbage and discard. Place the whole cabbage in the boiling water and cook until the first layers of leaves begin to soften and become pliable, enough to peel back without breaking off, about 5 minutes. Remove the head of cabbage carefully from the pot and peel back the tender leaves without tearing the leaves from the base. Allow the water to return to a boil, add the cabbage, and repeat the process (which will require less time to soften the leaves as you go), until the remaining center, or heart of the cabbage, is about the size of a tennis ball.

When the cabbage is cool enough to handle, remove this center with a sharp knife, being careful to keep the outer leaves attached to the base. Finely chop the cabbage heart and combine it with the beef and onion in a large mixing bowl. Add the herbs, bread crumbs, and eggs and season with salt and pepper.

Spread a 14-inch square of double-folded cheesecloth flat and place the cabbage in the center. Gently pull back the leaves and pack the stuffing into the center, being careful not to break the outer leaves. Fold the leaves back over the stuffing and wrap the cabbage in the cheesecloth, tying it closed with butcher twine.

Bring the cooking liquid back to a gentle boil. Carefully lower the cabbage into the stockpot. When the water returns to a boil, reduce the heat to simmer and cook for 1½ to 2 hours, until the filling is fully cooked (meat thermometer should read 160°F) and the cabbage is tender. Lift the cabbage from the pot, drain well, and remove and discard the cloth. Transfer the stuffed cabbage to a serving platter.

Drizzle the melted butter over the cabbage and then sprinkle with chopped parsley. Cut into wedges and serve.

CHEF'S NOTE

❦ This is not only one of Jefferson's favorite recipes, but also one of mine. It should be noted, however, that this recipe is not recommended for the beginner. The **blanching process** detailed above will take some time to master, but the extra attention and effort will result in an amazing dish.

BOUILLI (BOILED BEEF)

SERVES 8 TO 10

THOMAS JEFFERSON'S GRANDDAUGHTER, Ellen Coolidge, recalled in an 1856 letter: "He liked boiled beef, bouilli, better than roast." She felt that this preference, coupled with others that were "contrary to the custom of his countrymen," appeared to "his enemies as so many proofs of his being under French influence and conspiring with Bonaparte."

This recipe, a classic French beef dish, *was* a favorite of Thomas Jefferson's. There are several versions, and the earliest ones do not mention garlic, leeks, or herbs, but it's inconceivable that the French-trained cooks at Monticello would not have used them, so I've added them here. (See Bouillon Potatoes, page 158.)

- 3½ pounds beef rump roast or brisket
- 1 tablespoon kosher salt
- 1 teaspoon whole black peppercorns
- ½ teaspoon whole cloves
- 2 large sprigs each fresh parsley and thyme, tied into a bundle with kitchen twine
- 8 small white onions, peeled and left whole; or 4 medium onions, peeled and quartered
- 4 medium carrots, peeled and cut into 1-inch-long pieces
- 4 medium turnips, peeled and quartered
- 6 stalks celery with leafy greens, cut into 1-inch-long pieces
- 4 large or 6 small garlic cloves, lightly crushed, peeled, and left whole
- 4 small leeks, trimmed, cut in half lengthwise, and cleaned
- Horseradish Cream (page 247), optional

Put the beef into a large Dutch oven or stockpot, add the salt, and fill with enough water to cover the beef by about 2 inches.

Make a sachet by wrapping the peppercorns and cloves in cheesecloth and tie tight with butcher string. Add sachet and herb bundle to the stockpot and bring to a boil over medium heat. Cook until the meat is tender, 1½ to 2 hours, skimming off any foam that rises to the top.

Meanwhile, in a separate stockpot, combine the onions, carrots, turnips, celery, garlic, and leeks. Add enough liquid from the beef to cover the vegetables, and simmer for 30 to 45 minutes, until the vegetables are fork tender. This ragoût will be the base of the finished dish.

When the beef is tender, remove it from the pot and transfer to a platter. To serve, place a few vegetables on each plate. Slice the meat into ¼-inch-thick pieces and place over the vegetables. Top with some of the juices from the pot the vegetables were cooked in; serve immediately with Horseradish Cream if you like.

CHEF'S NOTE

- When choosing the **beef** from the butcher for this recipe, it is important to choose the cut with the most marbling present. During the 1½+ hours cooking time, the fat will combine and enhance the flavor of the beef as well as the vegetables.

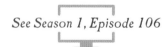

See Season 1, Episode 106

CHICKEN FRICASSEE

SERVES 4 TO 6

MRS. ELIZABETH HOUSE TRIST, also known as Eliza, became dear friends with Thomas Jefferson during his time with the Continental Congress when he lived at her mother's boardinghouse, from 1783 to 1784. Their friendship lasted throughout their lives; her grandson—Nicholas Trist—married Jefferson's granddaughter Virginia Randolph at Monticello. Mrs. Trist attributes her version of this recipe, originally titled A White Fricassee, to Virginia's mother, Martha Randolph. When I tested it though, I found that it needed a bit of an update. Aside from directing an extravagant waste of the cooking broth, her original recipe sacrifices flavor left and right for the sake of keeping a pristine whiteness in the dish.

I've therefore looked both to Mary Randolph's rendition of it in *The Virginia Housewife* (1828 edition) and to a later family recipe. Both recipes are superior in all respects to Mrs. Trist's and probably are more reflective of what the cooks did at Monticello.

- 1 small chicken (no more than 3 pounds), cut into 10 pieces (2 legs, 2 wings, 2 thighs, and 2 halved breasts)
- Kosher salt
- 2 cups whole milk
- 8 ounces small white mushrooms
- 1 cup heavy cream
- ½ teaspoon ground mace (preferably freshly ground)
- ½ to 1 teaspoon freshly grated nutmeg
- 4 tablespoons unsalted butter
- 2 tablespoons all-purpose flour
- ¼ cup dry white wine

Put the chicken pieces in a deep skillet or sauté pan with a tight-fitting lid. The pan should hold all of the chicken in one close-fitting layer. Pour boiling water over the chicken until it is completely covered. Cover the pan and allow the chicken to soak for 15 minutes. Strain and reserve the liquid. Rinse the chicken under cold running water.

Wipe out the pan and return the chicken to it. Sprinkle lightly with salt and pour the milk and enough of the reserved liquid over the chicken to cover it completely. Discard the remaining soaking liquid. Bring to a simmer over medium-low heat, cover the pan, and reduce the heat to barely simmering. Cook until the chicken is tender (internal temperature of 165°F), about 30 minutes.

While the chicken is cooking, wipe the mushrooms clean with a dry cloth. If the mushrooms are small leave them whole; if large, slice them into thick pieces.

Remove the chicken from the pan, cover, and keep warm. Strain the broth, wipe out the pan, and return 2 cups of the cooking broth to it. Stir in the cream, mace, and nutmeg and season with salt to taste. Bring it to a simmer over medium heat.

Meanwhile, knead together the butter and flour with your hands, or with a fork if you prefer. Bit by bit, stir it into the liquid and then simmer until slightly thickened.

Add the mushrooms and chicken to the pan and return to a simmer. Stir in the wine and cook until the mushrooms are just cooked through and the chicken is hot again, about 8 minutes. Transfer the chicken to a warm deep-rimmed serving platter, pour the sauce and mushrooms over it, and serve immediately.

CHEF'S NOTES

* If you discover that you do not have **mace** in your spice cupboard, simply increase the amount of nutmeg by ½ teaspoon.

* Thomas Jefferson would have a **chicken** taken from his estate and prepared immediately whenever he requested this dish. For those without access to live chickens, I have found that a kosher butcher shop has the freshest chicken prepared in a very similar manner to what would have been done at Monticello.

See Season 1, Episode 107

WEST INDIES CURRIED LAMB

SERVES 8

"CURRY POWDER IS USED as a fine flavoured seasoning for fish, fowl, steaks, chops, veal cutlets, hashes, minces, alamodes, turtle soup, and in all rich dishes, gravies, sauce, etc., etc." So wrote Mary Randolph, whose cookbook, *The Virginia Housewife*, includes recipes for curried fish, chicken, and rice. One normally wouldn't imagine curry being a part of the colonial culinary repertoire, but cooks, especially in seaport towns, were very familiar with the pungent blend of spices, as ships returning from the West Indies counted curry powder among the many commodities in their holds.

In the final episode of the four-part Monticello show, I wanted to create something spectacular and unique. Being in Jefferson's kitchen and cooking with Dr. Leni Sorensen was the opportunity of a lifetime, and I wanted to end the series with a spectacular dish. West Indies curried goat is an example of how global the cuisine of the eighteenth century could be— the curry from India with goat prepared with a distinctly Caribe twist ended up on the dinner tables at Monticello. *Overnight marinating is recommended.*

- 5 pounds boneless lamb shoulder, cut into 2-inch cubes
- 2 onions, diced
- 1 bunch scallions, diced
- ½ cup chopped garlic
- ½ cup minced peeled fresh ginger
- 1 cup curry powder
- 3 large fresh thyme sprigs
- ½ habanero pepper, seeded and finely chopped
- Kosher salt and freshly ground black pepper
- 1 cup dry red wine, such as Burgundy
- 4 tablespoons unsalted butter
- 1 carrot, peeled and diced
- 2 Roma tomatoes, diced

- 1 pound red potatoes, peeled and diced
- 3 quarts Chicken Stock (page 265 or store-bought)
- Chopped fresh parsley, for garnish

In a large bowl or casserole dish, combine the lamb, onions, scallions, garlic, ginger, curry powder, thyme, habanero, and salt and pepper. Pour the wine over the seasoned lamb, cover with plastic wrap, and marinate in the refrigerator, stirring occasionally, for at least 6 hours or overnight.

Remove the lamb from the marinade, reserving the marinade. Pat the lamb dry with paper towels. Melt the butter in a large Dutch oven over high heat, add the lamb, and sauté until the lamb is brown and the juices are reduced, 4 to 10 minutes, depending on preference.

Add the marinade and bring the mixture just to a boil over high heat. Reduce the heat to low, cover, and cook, stirring frequently, for 1½ hours.

Add the carrot, tomatoes, potatoes, and stock and continue to cook for 25 to 30 minutes, until the potatoes are al dente.

Before serving, discard the thyme sprigs and season the curry with salt and pepper to taste. Serve in a large serving bowl or deep platter, garnished with chopped parsley.

See Season 1, Episode 108

CHEF'S NOTE

♥ For this recipe we used lamb, but if you can find **bone-in goat**, that would make a spectacular rendition of this recipe. The method for preparing the dish remains the same, aside from butchering the goat with the bone kept in. When using goat, be aware that the bones have the potential to splinter, so look out for, and remove, any bone fragments in the finished dish.

SHRIMP IN SAFFRON CREAM

SERVES 4 TO 6

THOUGH THE BULK OF the world's saffron is grown in Spain, saffron was grown in England from medieval times until well past the eighteenth century in the Essex town of Saffron Walden. English settlers familiar with its many uses brought saffron to the colonies.

The golden spice requires an immense amount of labor to produce: the "threads" of saffron have to be handpicked from the crocus flower, and it takes approximately 150 flowers to produce a single gram of dried saffron. The extraordinary effort required for saffron has not changed much through history, which is why it remains one of the most expensive spices on the planet.

- 2 pounds jumbo shrimp, peeled and deveined
- ¼ cup Worcestershire sauce
- Juice of 1 lemon
- 4 tablespoons unsalted butter, at room temperature
- 1 medium shallot, finely chopped
- 1 cup sliced button mushrooms
- 1 cup dry white wine, such as Sauvignon Blanc
- 1 cup heavy cream
- Pinch of saffron threads
- 1 tablespoon all-purpose flour
- Kosher salt and freshly ground white pepper
- 2 tablespoons Pernod, or other anisette
- 1 tablespoon finely chopped parsley

Wash the shrimp thoroughly in cold running water and pat dry with paper towels. Combine the shrimp, Worcestershire sauce, and lemon juice in a mixing bowl and toss to coat. Cover and refrigerate for 1 hour.

Melt 3 tablespoons of the butter in a large skillet over medium heat. Add the shrimp and cook for 2 to 3 minutes per side, until completely pink. Remove and set aside.

Add the shallot to the skillet and sauté for 2 to 3 minutes, until translucent. Add the mushrooms and sauté until the liquid they release has evaporated, 5 to 8 minutes. Add the wine to deglaze the pan, stirring with a wooden spoon to loosen any browned bits on the bottom of the pan. Add the cream and saffron and cook for 5 to 8 minutes more, until the liquid in the pan is reduced by one-quarter.

In a small bowl, knead together the remaining 1 tablespoon butter and the flour to create a *beurre manié*, using your hands or mashing with a fork if you prefer. Whisk the *beurre manié* into the cream a little bit at a time, until the sauce is thick. Reduce the heat to low and return the shrimp to the skillet for a minute or two, just until warmed through. Season with salt and pepper to taste. Stir in the Pernod and parsley just before serving.

See Season 2, Episode 201

CORNMEAL-FRIED CATFISH

SERVES 4

IN THE EIGHTEENTH CENTURY, ponds or small lakes stocked with fish were very common features for grand estates, and James Madison's Montpelier was no exception; whenever he had the craving for catfish, he could have his chef get one right out of the pond. At the time, cornmeal was less expensive and more readily available than flour, which required more processing from the mill, and it was frequently used for battering fish.

- 4 catfish fillets, about 6 to 8 ounces each
- Juice of 1 lemon
- 1 teaspoon Worcestershire sauce
- Kosher salt and freshly ground black pepper
- ½ cup all-purpose flour
- 4 eggs, lightly beaten
- 1½ cups yellow cornmeal
- Vegetable oil, for frying

See Season 3, Episode 305

Place the catfish fillets in a 9 by 13-inch pan. Pour the lemon juice and Worcestershire sauce over the catfish and season with salt and pepper.

Place the flour, eggs, and cornmeal into separate dishes for dredging. Dip each catfish fillet first into the flour, then the egg, and then the cornmeal to evenly coat.

Place the coated catfish on a baking sheet and refrigerate until ready to fry.

Pour oil into a deep-fat fryer or 4-quart heavy saucepan to a depth of about 2 inches. Heat the oil over high heat to 350°F. (Check with a thermometer, or if you drop a small amount of cornmeal into the oil and it sizzles, it's hot enough.)

Fry the catfish (in batches, if necessary) for 5 minutes, until golden on both sides. Using a slotted spoon, remove the fish from the oil and place on a baking sheet lined with paper towels to absorb any excess oil. Serve immediately.

BAKED STUFFED STURGEON

SERVES 6 TO 8

GEORGE WASHINGTON WOULD HAVE fishermen catch sturgeon from the Potomac River on his estate, Mount Vernon. Sturgeon is a large, prehistoric-looking fish that still exists in our nation's waters. During Washington's lifetime, the common saying was that you could "walk across the Potomac River on the backs of sturgeon" due to the sheer number of them.

In Europe, sturgeon was classified as a royal fish that was reserved solely for the king's use. In the New World, this was not the case. The earliest settlers were shocked at the sight of Native Americans eating sturgeon and, without having had the opportunity to enjoy sturgeon in their homelands, were actually somewhat reluctant to do so. But they were soon convinced— sturgeon has a mild, yet unique flavor and its high oil content allowed for smoking and preserving. This recipe is based on one written by Mary Randolph, originally published in *The Virginia Housewife*.

- 2 pounds sturgeon, cut into 5- to 6-ounce fillets (or substitute mahi mahi)
- Kosher salt and freshly ground black pepper
- Crab Stuffing (page 252)
- 4 cups root vegetables, diced
- 2 cups white wine
- Juice of ½ lemon
- 8 tablespoons (1 stick) unsalted butter, cut into pieces
- 4 lemon wedges, for garnish
- Fresh chervil, for garnish
- Citrus Vinaigrette (page 250)

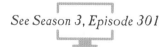
See Season 3, Episode 301

Preheat oven to 375°F.

Slice a horizontal pocket into each sturgeon fillet, being careful not to cut through to the other side. Season with salt and pepper.

Stuff the fillets with the crab stuffing and place a mound of stuffing on top for presentation.

Melt 2 tablespoons of butter and pour into a baking dish, then layer diced root vegetables along bottom of dish. Place the fillets in baking dish, pour the white wine and lemon juice over the fish, and dot with the remaining pieces of butter. Bake, allowing the fish to simmer in the wine sauce and basting occasionally, until white "pearls" of protein are present on top of fish, about 30 minutes.

Place the fillets on a platter and garnish with lemon wedges and chervil. Drizzle with citrus vinaigrette and serve immediately.

CHEF'S NOTES

❧ **Sturgeon**, unlike many other fishes, contains noticeable marbling in the flesh. I recommend looking for the fattiest cut available. Depending on where you live, sturgeon may be difficult to find (you may have to order it in advance from your fish market). If it is unavailable and you cannot find **mahi mahi**, ask someone at your fish market for suggestions of another mild-flavored firm-fleshed fish.

❧ This recipe would have only been available to the upper echelon of society as **citrus** had to be shipped in from Europe and, thus, was expensive. Washington's love of citrus is well documented; he would handwrite orders for a variety of citrus fruits and this meal would have been a regular at his home, Mount Vernon.

❧ I have added **tomato** to the recipe, in the vinaigrette, which was not commonly used until Jefferson helped make tomatoes more popular. With this rendition, I have taken creative liberty in enhancing the flavors with ingredients that were yet to become mainstream.

CURRIED SHRIMP AND TOFU

SERVES 4

TOFU HAS BEEN WIDELY enjoyed in Asia for centuries, possibly even millennia, but many find it quite surprising that tofu was also eaten in the New World in the eighteenth century. The cuisine of the colonial period is much more global than you may think, and Benjamin Franklin himself fell in love with Chinese tofu, which he inaccurately described as a type of cheese in a letter to John Bartram, the preeminent horticulturist in Philadelphia at the time:

> *London, January 11, 1770*
>
> *My ever-dear Friend: I send Chinese Garavances. Cheese [is] made of them, in China, which so excited my curiosity. Some runnings of salt (I suppose runnet) is put into water, when the meal is in it, to turn to curds. These…are what the Tau-fu is made of.*

While it was a noteworthy curiosity in Franklin's time, tofu has made a major impact on modern American cuisine in the last few decades and I believe that you will find working with this historic ingredient very enjoyable. This recipe is a perfect way to make tofu shine.

- 3 tablespoons sesame oil
- 2 teaspoons seeded and chopped fresh Thai pepper
- 4 garlic cloves, chopped
- 1 onion, sliced into half-moon shape
- 1 tablespoon chopped fresh ginger
- 1 teaspoon chopped fresh lemongrass
- 2 tablespoons curry powder

- 1 pound shrimp (15 to 20 per pound), peeled and deveined
- 1 cup dry white wine
- 1 cup heavy cream
- 6 baby bok choy, cut into quarters
- Kosher salt and freshly ground black pepper
- 20 ounces firm tofu, cut into large cubes
- ½ teaspoon Catchup to Last 20 Years (page 246) or fish sauce

Heat the sesame oil over high heat in a wok or large skillet. Add the Thai pepper, garlic, and onion and cook until the onion is translucent, about 3 minutes. Add the ginger, lemongrass, curry powder, and shrimp and cook for another 2 to 3 minutes, until the shrimp are fully cooked. Add the wine to the pan and deglaze, stirring with a wooden spoon to loosen any browned bits on the bottom of the pan; stir in the cream. Stir and add the bok choy with a little salt and pepper. Simmer for about 5 minutes, or until bok choy is tender but still bright in color and the sauce is thickened.

Remove from heat and gently fold in the tofu and the catchup, being careful not to break the tofu apart. Adjust seasoning, if necessary, and serve immediately.

CHEF'S NOTE

♥ Purchase the firmest **tofu** you can find. The packaging may specify "firm" or "very firm" or "extra firm." Be careful when incorporating the tofu into this dish, as broken or crumbled tofu will not look appealing.

See Season 3, Episode 303

VEAL KIDNEY DIJONNAISE

SERVES 4

FIRST LADY "DOLLEY" MADISON, the wife of our fourth president, James Madison, was a lover of French cuisine and considered a superb hostess who never failed to amaze. Her meals were legendary in the high-society circles of Virginia. In fact, her dinners were so enticing that even political rivals would enjoy themselves at her events without arguments—a unique situation for the time.

Mrs. Madison would present Veal Kidney Dijonnaise when she truly wished to impress, as the classic French preparation would have been reserved for the finest of occasions. Its popularity has not waned in Europe: to this day, you will find this dish on the menu at many upscale European restaurants and bistros.

- 2 veal kidneys, about 1 pound each
- Kosher salt and freshly ground black pepper
- 4 to 6 tablespoons clarified butter (see Chef's Note, page 17)
- ¾ cup chopped onion
- 2 cups sliced fresh mushrooms
- ¾ cup Madeira
- 1 cup heavy cream
- 1 cup Demi-Glace (page 263 or store-bought)
- 4 tablespoons unsalted butter, cut into pieces
- 3 tablespoons Dijon mustard
- 1 tablespoon fresh tarragon leaves, pulled from stem and left whole
- 1 tablespoon chopped fresh parsley

Prepare the kidneys by removing the fat from the outsides. Then remove the white membranes inside. Slice into small pieces (about ⅛ inch) and sprinkle with salt and pepper.

Heat the clarified butter in a skillet over high heat. Add the kidney pieces and cook, tossing, for about 2 minutes. Add the onion and cook for a minute. Add the mushrooms and sauté a minute more, until they are dry. Remove the mushrooms and kidneys from the pan and set aside.

Add the Madeira and then the cream to the pan. Stir in the demi-glace and season with pepper. Remove the pan from the heat and stir in the butter until incorporated. Stir in the mustard and tarragon. Return the kidney and mushrooms to the pan and stir to mix. Serve, garnished with minced parsley.

See Season 3, Episode 305

❦ **Kidney** is best served medium-rare. To prepare kidney to this temperature, it is best to use visual cues: as soon as the edges of the kidney begin to curl, it is medium-rare. Should you prefer a more well-done kidney, increase the cooking time until desired firmness is achieved.

❦ Do not discard the **fat** removed from the kidneys. In the eighteenth century, this was a precious ingredient because of its rich flavor. You can render the fat and use it in sauces or even in pie crusts for savory tarts.

ROASTED PHEASANT

SERVES 4 TO 6

THE PHEASANT IS A beautiful game bird that has been prized by hunters and chefs alike for centuries. In Europe, the hunting of pheasants was a wealthy man's pursuit, but in the New World no such rules existed, and they could be found in forests just outside of city limits.

Colonial cooks differentiated between male pheasants (cocks), female pheasants (hens), and young pheasants (poults). Hannah Glasse gives the following recommendations for choosing pheasants: "The spurs of the pheasant cock, when young, are short and dubbed; but long and sharp when old; when new, he has a firm vent, when stale, an open and flabby one." Pheasants were also always roasted with their heads on, turned toward the back for presentation.

Pheasants played a role in the friendship of George Washington and General Lafayette. Lafayette once gave Washington a gift of two partridges, three donkeys, and seven pheasants. The donkeys had been requested by Washington for use on his farmland, but the birds were a surprise. The pheasants came directly from King Louis XVI's aviary and Washington was quite touched by the gesture. Although most pheasants were considered game, these pheasants led a long and happy life as pets and were even preserved via taxidermy after they "made their exit"— as Washington put it. Two of the pheasants are still on display at Harvard. *Overnight marinating required.*

- 1 (750 ml) bottle dry red wine, such as Burgundy
- 6 whole peppercorns
- 1 bay leaf
- 1 sprig fresh thyme, plus thyme leaves for garnish
- 1 sprig fresh sage
- 2 (2½-pound) pheasants (or substitute chicken)
- 1 tablespoon dried sage
- 1 tablespoon dried thyme
- Kosher salt and freshly ground black pepper
- 4 cups Cornbread Stuffing (page 254)

- 1½ cups Demi-Glace (page 263 or store-bought)
- ¼ cup Rainwater Madeira (or regular Madeira)
- 2 tablespoons unsalted butter

To marinate the pheasants, combine the wine, peppercorns, bay leaf, thyme sprig, and sage sprig in a high-sided casserole dish. Add the pheasants and turn to coat. Cover and refrigerate overnight, turning periodically.

When ready to cook the pheasants, remove them from the marinade and pat dry with paper towels. Discard the marinade.

Preheat the oven to 425°F. Season the cavities with half of the dried sage and dried thyme, and salt and pepper to taste. Stuff the cavities with the stuffing, then tie the legs together with kitchen twine. Season the outsides of the pheasants with the remaining dried sage and dried thyme, and season with salt and pepper. Place the pheasants breast-up on a rack in a roasting pan.

Roast for 30 minutes, until the pheasants are browned, then baste with the pan drippings and cover with foil. Lower the oven temperature to 350°F and roast for an additional 45 minutes, until the thigh bones can be wiggled easily (internal temperature of 180°F). Remove from the oven and snip the twine from the legs.

Combine the demi-glace, pan drippings, Madeira, and butter in a small saucepan and cook over medium heat for 5 to 8 minutes, until completely warmed through. Place the pheasants on a large serving platter, top with the Madeira demi-glace, and garnish with thyme leaves.

CHEF'S NOTE

♥ For an added boost of flavor, add 3 tablespoons chopped **cranberries** to the stuffing.

See Season 3, Episode 306

CURRIED CHICKEN

SERVES 8

IN THE EIGHTEENTH CENTURY, this stew would have been made with goat or mutton because young chickens were rarely sacrificed; the eggs they laid were valuable. The curried chicken is inspired by Hannah Glasse's recipe for "Chicken Curry the Indian Way." Curry can be used with almost any meat or vegetable but, for many, chicken is the best protein for this spice mix. The bird's mild flavor absorbs the intricate blend of spices perfectly, making the dish one of my personal favorites. *Overnight marinating recommended.*

FOR THE CHICKEN AND MARINADE

- 1 (2- to 3-pound) chicken, cut into 16 pieces
- 1 large carrot, thinly sliced
- 1 large onion, chopped
- 3 garlic cloves, chopped
- ½ cup curry powder
- 4 cups (32 ounces) white wine

FOR THE CURRY

- 4 tablespoons unsalted butter
- 3 medium white onions, chopped
- 3 garlic cloves, chopped
- 3 bay leaves
- 1 large sprig fresh thyme
- ⅛ teaspoon cayenne pepper
- 1 cup heavy cream
- Kosher salt and freshly ground black pepper
- Chopped fresh parsley, for garnish

See Season 3, Episode 311

Marinate the chicken: In a large bowl or casserole dish, combine the chicken pieces, carrot, onion, garlic, and curry powder. Pour the wine over the mixture and cover with plastic wrap. Marinate in the refrigerator, stirring occasionally, at least 6 hours or overnight.

Make the curry: Remove the chicken pieces from the marinade, reserving the marinade. Pat the chicken dry with paper towels.

In a large Dutch oven, melt the butter over high heat. Add the chicken pieces and sauté for 8 to 10 minutes, until the chicken is brown and juices are reduced. Reduce the heat to medium and add the onions and garlic. Cook, stirring frequently, for about 10 minutes, until the onions are translucent. Add the reserved marinade, the bay leaves, thyme sprig, and cayenne and bring the mixture just to a boil over high heat. Reduce the heat to low, cover, and cook, stirring frequently, for about 45 minutes, until the chicken no longer appears pink (internal temperature of 165°F).

Add the cream and let simmer for 5 minutes to thicken the sauce. Before serving, discard the bay leaves and sprig of thyme. Season with salt and pepper to taste. Serve in a large serving bowl or deep platter. Garnish with the chopped parsley.

CHEF'S NOTES
---

* For the best results, use a fresh—never frozen—**chicken**.

* You can adjust the amount of **cayenne pepper** to customize the spice factor to your liking.

* When cooking with **curry powder**, carefully monitor your heat so the curry does not burn. Burnt curry has a very unpleasant flavor and can render a dish inedible.

* As with all dishes, be sure to use only fresh **garlic**. To my taste, jarred chopped garlic lacks the flavor of the real thing.

* You might want to **serve the curry** with Almond Rice Pilaf (page 165) and Mango Chutney (page 257).

TRIPE À LA MODE

SERVES 6 TO 8

THE COLONISTS WOULD HAVE brought their appetite for tripe from Europe, and those without the habit of eating tripe would have developed it as frugality was a key component of eighteenth-century cuisine. While tripe is not the favored delicacy it once was in the American colonies, this dish is one of my personal favorites. As a chef, I love working with tripe because of its versatility; it easily absorbs the flavors of the spices in whatever you are preparing and fits in perfectly with either a classic European dish or a spicy Asian soup.

FOR THE TRIPE

- 2½ pounds cleaned honeycomb tripe
- 1 tablespoon unsalted butter
- 1 tablespoon finely chopped garlic
- 1 tablespoon chopped shallot

FOR THE SAUCE

- 3 tablespoons unsalted butter
- 1 cup chopped shallots
- 3 tablespoons all-purpose flour
- 3 tablespoons Dijon mustard
- 4 cups Beef Stock (page 264 or store-bought)
- 2 cups Demi-Glace (page 263 or store-bought)
- ½ teaspoon white pepper
- Kosher salt
- ½ cup heavy cream
- ¼ cup dry white wine
- Chopped fresh chives, for garnish

Make the tripe: Bring a large saucepan of lightly salted water to a boil over high heat. Drop in the tripe and boil for 1 to 1½ hours (see Chef's Note). Remove the tripe, using a large slotted spoon, and set on paper towels to drain and cool slightly. Slice the cooled tripe into strips about 2 inches long and ⅛ inch wide.

Melt the butter in a large sauté pan over medium-low heat, toss in the garlic and shallot, and sauté until softened and translucent, but not brown. Add the tripe and cook until any liquid it releases has evaporated, about 3 minutes. Remove from the heat and set aside.

Make the sauce: Melt the butter in a sauté pan over medium heat. Add the 1 cup shallots and sauté until softened and translucent. Stir in the flour to make a smooth paste and remove the pan from the heat.

Whisk in the mustard, stock, and demi-glace. Season with the pepper and salt to taste and bring to a boil over high heat. Place the pan over medium heat and simmer until the sauce reduces by one-fourth, 8 to 10 minutes. Pour in the cream and simmer for 1 to 2 minutes longer.

To finish the dish, return the tripe to medium heat and add the wine to deglaze the pan, stirring with a wooden spoon to loosen any browned bits on the bottom of the pan, and simmer until warmed throughout.

Place the tripe on a serving platter and pour the sauce over it. Garnish with fresh chives and serve immediately.

> ——— CHEF'S NOTE ———
>
> ❦ **Tripe** will always come blanched (pre-cooked), but not all tripe is equal in size and thickness, so boiling time may vary. A typical piece will require between 1 and 1½ hours. Use a finger technique to determine doneness of your tripe: Pinch a piece of tripe in between your thumb and forefinger. If you are able to pinch through, the tripe is done! Pay close attention to the texture and degree of doneness while boiling the tripe. It will be difficult to eat if undercooked and will become too soft and mushy if overcooked.

See Season 4, Episode 401

NEW ENGLAND BOILED DINNER

SERVES 8 TO 10

IN *GOOD MAINE FOOD* (1939) by Marjorie Mosser, there is an excerpt from a 1775 journal entry in which the author describes the culinary habits of New Englanders: "In the evening before bedtime, the females of the house prepare the dinner of the following day. This was the manner: a piece of pork or beef, or a portion of each kind, together with a sufficiency of cabbage, potatoes, and turnips seasoned with salt, and an adequate quantity of water, were put into a neat tin kettle with a close lid. The kettle was placed on the stove in the room where we all slept, and there it simmered till the time of rising, when it was taken to a small fire in the kitchen where the stewing continued till near noon, when they dined…" This eighteenth-century slow cooking method is the classic boiled dinner.

New England is famous for so many of its contributions to America that I could spend an entire television season dedicated to this region and still leave the majority of stories untouched. The life and work of John Adams inspired me to take a trip to New England for a series of episodes. Of course, one simply cannot visit this beautiful area without enjoying a New England Boiled Dinner. While seafood certainly played a big role in the cuisine of the region, this recipe is a great example of the hearty comfort food.

- 4 pounds brisket of beef
- 1 pork shoulder (about 5 pounds)
- ¼ cup salt
- 6 whole black peppercorns
- 1 bay leaf
- 1 whole frying chicken (3 to 5 pounds)
- 3 parsnips, cubed
- 6 carrots, scraped
- 6 small white turnips, peeled
- 8 small white onions, peeled
- 3 or 4 golden beets, stems removed, cleaned, and peeled, then cut into six pieces each
- 4 small red potatoes, halved but not peeled
- 4 small yellow potatoes, halved but not peeled
- 2 or 3 leeks, cleaned and cut into 4-inch pieces
- 8 ounces Brussels sprouts, cleaned
- Chopped fresh parsley, for garnish

Place the beef and pork in a large stockpot and add enough water to cover the meat. Add the salt, peppercorns, and bay leaf and cover. Bring to a boil and simmer for 1½ hours, or until the meat is tender, skimming occasionally.

Add the chicken and cook for 30 to 45 minutes longer, until it is thoroughly cooked (internal temperature of 165°F). Remove the meat from the pot and keep in a warm oven while you cook the vegetables.

Add all the vegetables to the stock, bring to a gentle boil, and cook for 20 minutes, or until desired doneness. Using a slotted spoon, remove the vegetables and arrange on a platter; remove and discard the bay leaf.

To serve, slice the beef, pork, and chicken into pieces. Place the meat on a platter and arrange vegetables around. Sprinkle with chopped parsley and serve immediately.

CHEF'S NOTE

♥ I love making flavor really pop! My favorite way for this dish is to combine equal parts freshly **grated horseradish and grated beets** to serve alongside it.

See Season 4, Episode 403

GUYANESE DUCK CURRY

SERVES 4

GUYANA, NESTLED IN BETWEEN Venezuela to the west and Brazil to the south, is the only English-speaking country on the South American continent and famous for its rum production. It was the rum and Native American history that brought me to Guyana to shoot an episode for *A Taste of History,* and it was Guyana where I found a fascinating cuisine influenced by Native Americans, Dutch, British, Indians, and Africans.

Duck Curry is so ingrained in Guyana's culture that every household has its own recipe. Although variations are prepared all over the Caribbean, the Guyanese version is considered by many to be the best. This recipe is from a friend whose family has passed it down for generations.

- 1 whole duck (3 ½ to 5 pounds)
- ¼ cup oil
- 2 onions, coarsely chopped
- 6 garlic cloves, minced
- 2 tablespoons curry powder
- 4 plum tomatoes, coarsely chopped
- 1½ cups Duck Stock (page 266)
- 1 teaspoon garam masala
- 1 teaspoon toasted ground cumin (*chirra*, see Chef's Notes)
- 3 carrots, peeled and chopped
- 6 Yukon Gold potatoes, cut into pieces
- 1 tablespoon grated fresh ginger
- 1 bunch fresh thyme, leaves pulled from stems (stems discarded) and coarsely chopped
- 1 slice habanero pepper (about a tenth of a habanero), minced
- Kosher salt and freshly ground pepper

Butcher the duck into 16 pieces, or smaller. (Use the neck, back, wings, stomach, and other bits to make the duck stock.)

Heat the oil in a Dutch oven over medium heat. Add the onions, garlic, and curry powder and cook for 1 to 2 minutes, until lightly toasted. Watch carefully to avoid burning. Add the duck pieces and half the chopped tomatoes.

Pour the stock into the Dutch oven and bring to a simmer over medium heat. Cook for 5 to 6 minutes. Add the garam masala and cumin (*chirra*) and let cook another 5 minutes. Add the carrots, potatoes, ginger, thyme, and habanero pepper. Season with salt and pepper to taste. Cook slowly over low heat for about 30 minutes, or until duck pieces are tender (internal temperature of 170°F). Serve immediately.

CHEF'S NOTES

- To make *chirra*, which is a popular spice in Guyana, toast whole cumin seeds lightly in a pan and then grind them in a spice grinder or mortar and pestle.

- When handling **habanero peppers**, always remember to wear gloves and thoroughly wash your hands after handling them. If you are a fan of heat, increase the amount of habanero to your preference.

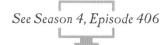

See Season 4, Episode 406

COQ AU VIN ROUGE

SERVES 4

My COQ AU VIN recipe specifies *rouge*, which may seem redundant as the most commonly prepared coq au vin recipes call for red wine. In Europe, however, now and throughout history, coq au vin could be made with either a white wine, such as Riesling, or with a red, such as a Burgundy or pinot noir.

The white wine version was most popular around Alsace, whereas the red wine–producing regions of France were more likely to use Burgundy. While both are wonderful dishes, the red wine version is now the most popular and my preferred method. *Overnight marinating required.*

- 1 (750 ml) bottle red wine
- 2 onions, chopped; plus another 1 cup chopped for the pot
- 4 garlic cloves, chopped; plus 1 tablespoon minced for the pot
- 3 sprigs fresh rosemary
- 3 sprigs fresh thyme, stems removed, plus more leaves for garnish
- Freshly ground black pepper
- 1 chicken (3 to 5 pounds), cut into 8 pieces
- Kosher salt
- ½ cup all-purpose flour
- 4 tablespoons unsalted butter or vegetable oil
- About 3 cups Chicken Stock (page 265 or store-bought)
- 4 ounces bacon, diced
- 2 cups button mushrooms
- 1 cup pearl onions

In a large bowl, combine 2 cups of the red wine with the 2 cups onions, chopped garlic, rosemary, thyme, and pepper to taste. Stir to combine. Add the chicken pieces and cover. Marinate the chicken overnight in the refrigerator.

Remove the chicken from the marinade and discard the marinade. Pat the chicken dry and season with salt and pepper. Place the flour in a shallow dish, dredge the chicken pieces thoroughly in the flour, and set them on a baking sheet.

Melt the butter (or heat the oil) in a large Dutch oven or heavy-bottomed soup pot over medium heat. Add the chicken and brown on all sides, turning the pieces as they cook to ensure even browning.

When the chicken is nicely browned, add the 1 cup chopped onion and the minced garlic; stir and cook for 3 to 5 minutes, until the vegetables become fragrant but not browned. Add the remaining red wine (about 1 cup) and deglaze, stirring with a wooden spoon to loosen any browned bits on the bottom of the pan.

Add enough stock to cover the chicken and bring to a boil over high heat. Reduce immediately to low heat and cook at a simmer for 35 to 45 minutes, until the chicken is completely cooked and tender (internal temperature of 165°F).

Meanwhile, place the bacon in a pot and cover with water. Bring to a boil over high heat and cook for 2 minutes. Drain. Cook the bacon in a medium saucepan over low heat for 5 to 7 minutes. Add the mushrooms and pearl onions and sauté until the onions are translucent and the mushrooms are browned.

Add the bacon, mushroom, and pearl onion mixture to the pot with the chicken and broth. Bring to a simmer and cook for 10 minutes. Garnish with fresh thyme and serve immediately.

CHEF's NOTES

- Do not be alarmed by the **color** of the chicken while preparing this recipe. The red wine will "stain" the chicken while cooking.

- Boiling (or blanching) **bacon** may sound strange, but it helps render the fat quickly and the bacon will reach the desired crispness more quickly using this method.

- This dish is typically served with **egg noodles** but another good choice would be mashed potatoes.

See Season 5, Episode 503

BEEF ROYALE

SERVES 6 TO 8

I CREATED THIS RECIPE in honor of an important figure in history, Bishop William White. The name may not be familiar to many, but in the eighteenth century, bishops were powerful figures politically and socially. Bishop White gave his sermons at Christ Church in Philadelphia and his congregants included George Washington and Benjamin Franklin, among many other noted individuals.

Bishop White's house has been left as it was during his lifetime and is now maintained by the National Park Service. This decadent dish, with its truffles, oysters, and beef marrow, would have suited Bishop White's taste; he was famously passionate about food and considered by many to be a true gourmet.

- 1 New York strip loin (4 to 5 pounds)
- ⅛ teaspoon freshly ground mace
- Freshly grated nutmeg
- ¼ teaspoon freshly ground cloves
- Kosher salt and freshly ground black pepper
- 5 tablespoons unsalted butter
- 1 small yellow onion, chopped (about ½ cup)
- 3 cups chanterelle mushrooms
- 1 cup thinly sliced white button mushrooms
- ½ cup dried porcini mushrooms
- 1 tablespoon thinly sliced black truffle, optional
- ⅓ cup Rainwater Madeira (or regular Madeira)
- ¼ cup thinly sliced beef marrow
- 2 cups Demi-Glace (page 263 or store-bought)
- Cornmeal-Fried Oysters (recipe follows), chopped
- ¼ cup sliced gherkin pickles
- 2 tablespoons chopped anchovies
- 3 tablespoons vegetable oil

Preheat oven to 350°F.

Trim the fat from the strip loin, leaving a thin layer (about ⅛-inch thick) for moisture. Season the beef with the mace, nutmeg, cloves, and salt and pepper.

Melt 3 tablespoons of the butter in a large Dutch oven over high heat. Add the strip loin and sear on both sides until browned and caramelized, about 5 minutes per side. Cover the Dutch oven and roast in the oven until the internal temperature of the meat is 130°F, about 50 minutes. Let rest 15 to 20 minutes.

Meanwhile, melt the remaining 2 tablespoons butter in a skillet over medium heat. Add the onion and sauté until translucent,

2 to 4 minutes. Add the chanterelles, button mushrooms, dried porcini, and truffle, stir gently to combine, and cook for 1 minute.

To deglaze the pan, add the Madeira and stir with a wooden spoon to release any brown bits from bottom of pan. Add the bone marrow and 1 cup demi-glace and simmer for 10 minutes, until the mushrooms are just tender.

In a separate saucepan, heat the remaining 1 cup demi-glace to a low simmer; it will be served over the finished dish.

Slice the rested strip loin into ¼-inch-thick slices.

Prepare the filling by gently combining the fried oysters, gherkins, anchovies, and oil in a mixing bowl. Place about 1 tablespoon of the filling on each slice of strip loin; roll into log shapes. Serve the rolls over the mushrooms and drizzle with remaining warmed demi-glace.

See Season 5, Episode 510

CORNMEAL-FRIED OYSTERS

- ¼ cup cornmeal
- 2 tablespoons all-purpose flour
- Pinch of kosher salt and freshly ground black pepper
- 1 tablespoon unsalted butter
- 12 oysters, purchased shucked with their liquor

Combine the cornmeal, flour, and salt and pepper in a shallow bowl.

Heat the butter in a large skillet over medium-high heat until sizzling hot.

Dredge each oyster in the cornmeal mixture and drop into the sizzling butter. Cook, turning once, until golden on all sides, about 1 minute. Remove with slotted spoon and drain on paper towels.

CHEF'S NOTE

- While delicious, the **truffle** is not mandatory for this recipe. If one is difficult to find, don't worry: you can omit it. The dish will still be spectacular.

VEAL TONGUE FRICASSEE

SERVES 4 TO 6

NOT WILLING TO WASTE one single part of an animal after the slaughter, eighteenth-century cooks developed many recipes for tongue. It was pickled, roasted, stuffed, stewed, potted, and even rubbed with charcoal to preserve it in the same manner as Westphalia ham.

Luckily, we have amazingly detailed records of the dining habits of the era that I have been able to use as research material. It is the attention to detail of our ancestors that has allowed food history to exist as it does today.

Thomas Jefferson employed a French maître d'hotel named Etienne Lemaire. Mr. Lemaire kept detailed shopping lists and recorded Jefferson's dining habits in a diary. Through his work, I am able to say that Jefferson would have been quite fond of this recipe. While I have crafted the recipe for use as a main course, Jefferson most often enjoyed beef and veal tongue as a breakfast food.

- 2 pounds veal tongue
- 4 tablespoons unsalted butter
- 1 cup diced carrots
- 1 cup diced onion
- 1 cup diced potatoes
- 1 cup diced rutabaga
- 1 pound mixed wild mushrooms, such as cremini, wood ear, and portobello
- 2 cups white wine
- 1 cup cream

See Season 5, Episode 511

Scrub the tongue thoroughly under running water. Place in a large stockpot with enough water to cover completely and bring just to a boil over medium-high heat. Reduce the heat to medium and cook for about 1 hour, until the tip of the tongue can be penetrated when squeezed (see Chef's Notes).

Remove the tongue from the pot and allow to cool until it can be handled. Peel the tongue while it is still warm, removing the white outer part.

In a separate saucepan, melt the butter over medium heat. Add the carrots, onion, potatoes, and rutabaga and sauté for about 10 to 15 minutes, or until the vegetables release their juices.

Add the mushrooms and cook for 10 to 15 minutes longer, until they darken, become glossy, and begin to release liquid. Add the wine and stir with a wooden spoon to deglaze the pan, loosening any browned bits on the bottom. Add the tongue and sautéed vegetables and simmer for 5 to 10 minutes. Add the cream and return to a simmer. Continue to simmer until the liquid is reduced and thickened, about 5 minutes.

Place the vegetables on a platter, top with the tongue and then the sauce; serve immediately.

CHEF'S NOTES

❧ Basically, the **finger technique** means squeezing the tip of the tongue. If you are able to penetrate, or break through, the meat in this fashion, that is a good sign the tongue is cooked through.

❧ In this recipe, slice the **tongue** lengthwise.

SHRIMP AND RUTABAGA FRICASSEE

SERVES 6 TO 8

RUTABAGAS WERE VERY COMMON in colonial gardens: they wintered well and were easily grown. Shrimp, on the other hand, do not hold up well with traveling or storage and would have been available only to those who lived in a coastal area. This recipe is a bit time-consuming, but well worthwhile for a cook who has a desire to serve a truly unforgettable dinner.

- 3 rutabagas, peeled and sliced into wedges
- 4 tablespoons unsalted butter
- 1 onion, diced
- 2 pounds shrimp (15–20 per pound), peeled and deveined
- 2 tablespoons minced anchovies
- Freshly grated nutmeg
- 1 cup shrimp stock (see Chef's Notes)
- 1 pinch saffron
- 2 tablespoons fish sauce (or Catchup to Last 20 Years, page 246)
- ½ cup sherry
- ½ cup heavy cream
- 1 lemon, halved
- Chopped fresh chives, for garnish
- Fresh tarragon leaves, for garnish
- Pinch red pepper flakes

Using a paring knife, shape each wedge of rutabaga into an ellipse, like a football. Place the rutabaga ellipses in a large saucepan, cover with cold water, and season with salt. Bring just to a boil then reduce the heat and simmer for 10 to 15 minutes, until tender. Remove the rutabaga with a slotted spoon and set aside.

In a separate stockpot, melt the butter over medium heat. Add the onion and cook until translucent, about 5 minutes. Add the shrimp, anchovies, and a little freshly grated nutmeg. Add the shrimp stock, stir to combine, and add the saffron. Simmer over low heat for 5 to 8 minutes, until the shrimp is just pink and cooked through.

Add the cooked rutabagas, fish sauce, sherry, and cream. Let sit over low heat for a minute or two for the flavors to marry. Squeeze half the lemon over the mixture and garnish with chives and tarragon. Sprinkle with red pepper flakes and serve immediately.

CHEF'S NOTES

- The **shrimp stock** is not mandatory for this recipe; it simply adds an extra boost of flavor to the dish. You can substitute vegetable stock.

- Frozen peeled and deveined **shrimp** may be used in place of fresh shrimp with similar results.

See Season 6, Episode 604

STUFFED LOBSTER

SERVES 2

IT'S SURPRISING TO SEE such a worldly man as Benjamin Franklin write a recipe for lobster, since it was commonly an ingredient reserved only for the poorest of people or servants. He was a man of considerable means and was not one to spare expense when it came to dining. Perhaps he was ahead of his time in appreciating the delicious ways in which lobster can be enjoyed.

In this recipe, cooked lobster meat is cleaned from the shell, combined with the other ingredients, and then stuffed back into the shell to finish in the oven.

FOR THE LOBSTER

- ⍅ 1 large (2½-pound) live lobster, split in half lengthwise
- ⍅ 2 cups fresh crumbs from Sally Lunn Bread (page 194)
- ⍅ 8 tablespoons (1 stick) unsalted butter, melted
- ⍅ 2 tablespoons lemon juice
- ⍅ 1 teaspoon Dijon mustard
- ⍅ 1 teaspoon cayenne pepper
- ⍅ 1 teaspoon kosher salt
- ⍅ 1 teaspoon freshly ground black pepper

FOR THE SHERRY CREAM SAUCE

- ⍅ 3 tablespoons unsalted butter
- ⍅ 4 shallots, minced
- ⍅ 2 cups button mushrooms
- ⍅ ½ cup sherry
- ⍅ ½ cup heavy cream

See Season 6, Episode 609

Preheat oven to 375°F.

Make the lobster: Fill a large stockpot with enough water to fully submerge the lobster and bring to a boil. Add the lobster and boil until the meat begins to separate from the shell, 5 to 10 minutes. Remove the lobster and drain, allowing it to cool slightly.

Remove the lobster meat from the tail and body, pulling it apart into coarse chunks, and place in a large mixing bowl. Claws are left whole and set aside. Add the bread crumbs, melted butter, lemon juice, mustard, cayenne pepper, salt, and black pepper to the lobster meat and gently fold the ingredients together until just combined. Spoon the stuffing back into the lobster shell. Place on a baking sheet and bake until warmed through, about 15 minutes.

Make the sherry cream sauce: Meanwhile, melt the butter in a small saucepan over low heat. Add the shallots and cook until translucent, 5 to 7 minutes. Add the mushrooms and cook until lightly browned, another 5 to 7 minutes. Add the sherry and deglaze, stirring with a wooden spoon to loosen any browned bits on the bottom of the pan. Stir in the cream and simmer until the sauce is thick enough to coat the back of a spoon.

Place the stuffed lobster on a serving platter and pour the cream sauce over it; serve immediately.

CALF LIVERS in CALVADOS

SERVES 4

THIS IS A CLASSIC French dish that is popular in regions where apples grow, using both fresh Granny Smith apples and Calvados, a brandy made from distilling apples down to their essence. Calf livers are still popular in France, as they were in eighteenth-century America, though they may be a bit of an acquired taste for modern Americans. Even if you have never been a fan of liver, this recipe might change your mind.

- 1 cup all-purpose flour
- Pinch of freshly grated nutmeg
- Kosher salt and freshly ground black pepper
- 8 slices calf liver (3 to 4 ounces each)
- 8 tablespoons (1 stick) unsalted butter
- 1 cup Calvados brandy
- ½ cup Demi-Glace (page 263 or store-bought)
- 1 pound Granny Smith apples, peeled, cored, and thinly sliced

In a shallow dish, mix together the flour, nutmeg, and a pinch each salt and pepper. Dredge the liver pieces in the flour.

Melt 4 tablespoons of the butter in a skillet over high heat. Add the dredged liver pieces and sear on both sides until browned, about 1 minute per side, which cooks them thoroughly.

Add ½ cup of the Calvados to the pan, stirring with a wooden spoon to loosen any browned bits on the bottom of the pan, then leave over medium heat until warmed. Transfer the meat to a serving platter.

Heat the demi-glace in a medium saucepan. Add the remaining 4 tablespoons

butter. When the butter is sizzling, add the apples and sauté until lightly cooked. Add the remaining ½ cup Calvados and deglaze, stirring with a wooden spoon to loosen any browned bits on the bottom of the pan.

Place the apples on the platter with the liver and lightly drizzle a ribbon of sauce over one edge of the liver. Serve immediately.

CHEF'S NOTES

- **Calf liver** can be found in gourmet grocery stores or artisan butcher shops.

- **Calvados** is a brandy made by distilling apple cider into a liquor, and also the name of an area within the Normandy region of France. The brandy predates the region: there are recipes for apple cider brandy that date back into the Napoleonic times (Napoleon kept Calvados on the ships of his navy for use as an antiseptic agent and for anesthetic purposes), but the region Calvados was only named *after* the French Revolution.

See Season 6, Episode 610

FRIED SWEETBREADS

SERVES 4 TO 6

EVER-FRUGAL COLONIAL HOUSEWIVES learned to make sweetbreads in all manner of ways. In *The Art of Cookery, Made Plain and Easy*, Hannah Glasse advises readers that "there are many ways of dressing sweetbreads: you may lard them with thin strips of bacon and roast them with what sauce you please; or you may marinate them, cut them into thin slices, flour them and fry them."

Offal meats require a bit of effort, but the additional work creates a remarkable end result. Fried sweetbreads have a subtler flavor than most other offal cuts and the crispy outside complements the beautiful firm but tender texture of the sweetbread.

I created this recipe while exploring the life of Dr. Benjamin Rush. This famous doctor, considered the father of American psychiatry, was also an epicurean with a sophisticated palate. He lived across the street from Alexander Hamilton, and together they would have enjoyed indulging in fried sweetbreads at their elaborate dinners.

- 1 onion, quartered
- 2 bay leaves
- 2 to 2½ pounds sweetbreads
- 2 cups all-purpose flour
- 1 teaspoon kosher salt
- 1 teaspoon white pepper
- ¼ teaspoon cayenne pepper
- 3 to 4 eggs
- 3 cups fresh bread crumbs
- 1 to 2 quarts vegetable oil
- Lemon slices
- Herbed Rémoulade (page 262)
- Chopped fresh parsley, for garnish

Fill a large stockpot with enough water to cover the sweetbreads and bring to a low boil over medium-high heat. Add the onion and bay leaves. Add the sweetbreads and poach until firm, 5 to 8 minutes. Remove from the heat and allow the sweetbreads to cool in the water.

In three separate bowls, set up your breading station: In one bowl, mix the flour, salt, white pepper, and cayenne pepper. Lightly beat the eggs in the second, and place the bread crumbs in the third.

Fill a stockpot between one-third and one-half full with oil and heat to 350°F.

Remove the cooled sweetbreads from the water and cut into ¼-inch slices. Pat them dry, then coat in the flour, dip in the eggs, and finally coat with the bread crumbs.

Add the sweetbreads in batches of 2 to 4 slices at a time to the oil and fry until golden brown, 3 to 5 minutes per batch. Remove with a slotted spoon and drain on paper towels. Serve with lemon slices, rémoulade, and chopped parsley.

Chef's Notes

- The **sweetbreads** are finished poaching when they become firm to the touch.
- **Bread crumbs** should be made at home or purchased at your local bakery. Avoid store-bought bread crumbs, as they can contain unwanted spices and seasonings. Do not use panko crumbs for this recipe.

See Season 7, Episode 703

SAUERBRATEN

SERVES 6 TO 8

ALTHOUGH ASSOCIATED WITH GERMANY, sauerbraten-like recipes date back to Julius Caesar, when he sent clay jugs, or *amphoras*, containing wine-pickled meat to the newly established Roman colony of Cologne. Throughout history, a variety of meats have been used for this dish, but it is now almost exclusively made with beef.

Sauerbraten is not a quick recipe; it requires time and attention (start the first steps three to five days in advance), but it is worth it and can be accomplished at home by cooks of all skill levels.

FOR THE BEEF AND MARINADE

- 4 cups white vinegar
- 4 cups red wine
- 2 large carrots, cut into large dice
- 2 large onions, cut into large dice
- 1 large stalk celery, cut into large dice
- 1 small celery root (celeriac), peeled and cut into large dice
- 2 tablespoons pickling spice
- ½ cup juniper berries
- ½ teaspoon ground ginger
- 3 bay leaves
- 1 tablespoon freshly ground black pepper
- 1 (3-pound) chuck roast

See Season 8, Episode 805

FOR THE SAUERBRATEN

- Kosher salt and freshly ground black pepper
- 1 large carrot, cut into large dice
- 1 large white onion, cut into large dice
- 2 large stalks celery, cut into large dice
- 4 cups dry red wine
- 4 tablespoons unsalted butter
- ¼ cup all-purpose flour

Marinate the beef: Combine all ingredients, except the chuck roast, in a large stainless-steel stockpot and bring to a boil over high heat. Cook at a high simmer for 15 minutes; remove from the heat and let the mixture cool.

Add the chuck roast to the cooled marinade, cover, and refrigerate for 3 to 5 days. (It's best to marinate in a nonreactive container like a stainless-steel stockpot.)

Cook the sauerbraten: Heat a large Dutch oven over high heat.

Remove the meat from the marinade and pat dry (discard the marinade). Season the roast with salt and pepper. Add to the hot Dutch oven and sear on both sides until well

browned. Add the carrot, onion, celery, and wine. Cover and cook over low to medium-low heat for 1 hour, or until the meat is tender. Remove the roast from the liquid and let it rest on a platter under a loose foil tent while you finish the gravy.

Knead the butter and flour together into a smooth paste, using your hands or a fork. Add to the pot and cook over low heat, stirring to thicken the gravy, about 8 minutes.

Slice the meat into ¼-inch-thick slices, cutting against the grain. Place on a serving platter and top with gravy. Serve immediately.

CHEF'S NOTES

- Do not be alarmed by the **color** of the roast after marinating. The red wine will give the meat a deep color.

- A **beurre manié**, which means "kneaded butter" in French, is equal parts of flour and butter mixed together. When mixing the flour and butter, it is imperative that the butter is soft enough to achieve an even mixture.

FRIED SOFT-SHELL CRABS

SERVES 6

CRAB, LIKE LOBSTER, WAS so plentiful in the New World that it was often used as bait, in addition to being prepared in all manner of dishes, including crab cakes, crab soup, and crab stuffing (page 252). For those who live outside the Mid-Atlantic states, soft-shell crabs may seem like an exotic item, but they are just common blue crabs that molt their hard, outer shell in May, and are caught before their new shells harden. The shell is so tender, the cooked crab is eaten whole.

- Vegetable oil, for frying
- 4 cups all-purpose flour
- Kosher salt and freshly ground black pepper
- 6 eggs
- 4 cups fresh bread crumbs
- 1 dozen soft-shell crabs (see Chef's Notes), cleaned
- Herbed Rémoulade (page 262), optional

Fill a medium-large stockpot one-third full with oil and heat to 375°F.

In three separate bowls, set up a breading station: In one bowl mix the flour, salt, and pepper. Lightly beat the eggs in the second; and place the bread crumbs in the third. Dredge each crab in the seasoned flour, dip in the beaten eggs, then coat with bread crumbs.

Place the crabs in the hot oil one at a time, being careful not to overcrowd the pot, and fry for 4 minutes. Using tongs, flip the crabs over and fry for an additional 4 minutes, until golden brown. Cook in batches if necessary.

Remove the crabs from the pot, allow to drain in a colander lined with paper towels, and serve with the rémoulade, if desired.

CHEF'S NOTES

- **Soft-shell crabs** should be available at most grocery stores or at a specialty seafood store when in season. Purchase them cleaned, for convenience.

- **Bread crumbs** should be made at home or purchased at your local bakery. Avoid store-bought bread crumbs, as they contain unwanted spices and seasonings. *Do not use panko crumbs.*

See Season 8, Episode 807

FRIED RABBIT

SERVES 6 TO 8

IN THE EIGHTEENTH CENTURY, the Northeast was rich with all kinds of small game, including wild rabbits and hare. Together with turkey, venison, and other game, rabbits served as another free food source for the colonists, who took full advantage of it. Rabbits in particular were incredibly common and, thus, enjoyed by all segments of society.

During the Revolutionary War, soldiers would often be far from home; sometimes in places that were completely unfamiliar to them. Despite the ever-changing landscape that soldiers experienced while marching to a battle, there was one thing that would remain constant: rabbits. During the moments between fighting, troops could wander into the woods or fields and secure fresh rabbit for dinner. Enjoyed by colonists at home and on the battlefield, fried rabbit was a meal that helped fuel the Revolution.

- Vegetable oil, for frying
- 4 cups all-purpose flour
- 2 tablespoons ground white pepper
- 2 tablespoons paprika
- 1 tablespoon rubbed sage
- 1 tablespoon kosher salt
- 1 tablespoon cayenne pepper
- 2 whole rabbits (about 2 pounds each), cut into 8 pieces each

See Season 8, Episode 809

In a large Dutch oven or stockpot, add enough oil to fill the pot one-third full and heat to 375°F.

Mix together the flour and spices in a large bowl, combining thoroughly. Dredge the rabbit pieces in the flour mixture, ensuring an even coating.

In batches of 5 or 6 pieces at a time and without crowding the pot, carefully place the dredged rabbit pieces into the hot oil with a slotted spoon. Fry for 10 to 12 minutes, until the rabbit is golden brown (it will float to the top when it is thoroughly cooked). Using tongs or a slotted spoon, remove the rabbit from the oil and set on a baking sheet lined with paper towels to drain briefly. Then arrange on a platter and serve immediately.

BRAISED LAMB SHANKS

SERVES 4

WHEN THOMAS JEFFERSON WANTED to escape the city of Philadelphia for a breath of fresh air, he would often join his friend Charles Thomson at Harriton House in Bryn Mawr.

The trip was a fifteen-mile journey; Jefferson would ride by horseback from his home at Seventh and Market Street in Philadelphia to Harriton House. As a result, Jefferson would often stay for long weekends. It was not just the change of scenery that inspired these trips, though. Jefferson and Thomson shared many stances including the abolition of slavery, which was a radical concept at the time. While lamb would have been out of reach for many during the eighteenth century—sheep were valuable livestock because the production of wool was important—Thomson and Jefferson would have enjoyed lamb dishes, such as this recipe, while relaxing in the Pennsylvania countryside.

Charles Thomson is a name that may be less familiar than other Founding Fathers such as Franklin, Washington, and Jefferson, but his contributions were just as significant. He was the original secretary of the Continental Congress—succeeded by George Washington. At the time, this position was considered by some as the equivalent of the "Prime Minister of America."

- ¼ cup vegetable oil
- 4 lamb hind-shanks
- Kosher salt and freshly ground black pepper
- 1 white onion, cut into 1-inch dice
- 2 tablespoons minced garlic (about 4 cloves)
- 2 cups dry red wine, such as Burgundy
- 3 cups Demi-Glace (page 263 or store-bought)
- 1 sprig fresh rosemary
- 2 sprigs fresh thyme
- 2 rutabagas, peeled and cut into 1-inch dice

- 2 parsnips, peeled and cut into 1-inch dice
- 2 large carrots, peeled and cut into 1-inch dice
- 1 celery root (celeriac), peeled and cut into 1-inch dice

Preheat oven to 375°F.

Heat the oil in a large Dutch oven or stockpot set over high heat.

Season the lamb shanks with salt and pepper, add them to the oil and sear on all 4 sides until golden brown, 3 to 4 minutes per side, for a total of 12 to 15 minutes.

Using tongs, transfer the browned lamb shanks to a platter. Add the onion and garlic to the pot and cook over medium heat until the onions become translucent and the edges just begin to brown. Return the lamb to the Dutch oven and add the red wine, stirring with a wooden spoon to loosen any browned bits on the bottom of the pan. Add the demi-glace, rosemary, and thyme. Cover, and bake in the oven for 45 minutes.

Add the rutabagas, parsnips, carrots, and celery root to the pot. Return the pot to the oven and bake uncovered for another 25 to 30 minutes, until the shanks are tender (internal temperature about 145°F for medium-rare, or up to 170°F for well-done). About 1 or 2 inches of the bone will be exposed.

Remove the sprigs of rosemary and thyme, adjust seasoning as desired, and transfer the lamb shanks to a platter. Arrange the vegetables with any juices around the meat and serve immediately.

See Season 9, Episode 910

BRAISED BLUEFISH

SERVES 4 TO 6

I AM OF THE OPINION that bluefish is criminally underrated today. While some restaurants have begun to feature it, it is uncommon, and a lot of home cooks shy away from it as well. Braising really opens up the natural flavors of the fish. I have absolutely fallen in love with the combination of fennel and bluefish. The subtle anise-like flavor of the fennel pairs with the boldness of the bluefish to create a complex flavor profile that could be described as bright or spring-like.

Thomas Jefferson was introduced to fennel by his neighbor, Philip Mazzei, a Florentine émigré and fellow plant enthusiast. Jefferson noted: "The fennel is beyond every other vegetable, delicious. It greatly resembles in appearance the largest size celery, perfectly white, and no vegetable equals it in flavour."

- 8 ounces bacon, cut into small dice
- 1 medium onion, cut into small dice
- 2 tablespoons minced garlic
- 4 small heads fennel, bulb only, sliced ¼ inch thick
- Kosher salt and freshly ground black pepper
- 2 cups white wine
- 4 to 6 (6-ounce) bluefish fillets
- 5 to 6 teaspoons Dijon mustard
- 6 tablespoons unsalted butter, cut into 4 to 6 pieces
- 2 cups fresh bread crumbs

Preheat oven to 375°F. Grease a baking pan that is large enough to hold the fish in a single layer.

In a large skillet over medium heat, slowly render the bacon, cooking for 3 to 5 minutes. Add the onion and garlic and cook for another 2 minutes, or until translucent but not browned. Add the fennel and sauté for 8 minutes, or until slightly softened. Season with salt and pepper. Add the wine and simmer.

Distribute the fennel mixture evenly in the greased baking pan. Season the fish fillets with a little salt and pepper, place on top of the fennel, and brush with mustard. Top each fillet with bread crumbs and a piece of butter.

Bake for 25 to 30 minutes, until golden brown. Serve immediately.

CHEF'S NOTES

- You can easily substitute other fatty fish, such as mackerel or salmon, for the **bluefish**.

- **Bread crumbs** should be made at home or purchased at your local bakery. Avoid store-bought bread crumbs, as they contain unwanted spices and seasonings. *Do not use panko crumbs.*

- **Dijon mustard** is particularly important for this recipe for its tangy qualities and specific spices. Avoid using other styles of mustard such as yellow, spicy brown, etc.

See Season 8, Episode 810

ELK STEW

SERVES 8 TO 10

WHEN WILLIAM PENN WAS granted the land that would later become Pennsylvania, he did not want to live in luxurious isolation; he wanted to bring people from all over the world to this new land. He wanted to create a better society than humankind had been able to achieve thus far in history.

To attract new residents, he advertised in Europe. One of the biggest selling points was not the fact that it was an unprecedented social experiment, but rather, the amazing hunting. But it was not just the "noble beasts" such as elk that were available, but also all manner of animal, from rabbit to deer. In addition to the rich wildlife, there was a wealth of wild berries and a wide array of edible mushrooms. The flora and fauna of the New World enticed many Europeans to make the journey.

This rich and elegantly simplistic stew is an example of how Penn and other early settlers would have enjoyed the elk they were able to freely hunt in the New World.

- 3 tablespoons olive oil
- 2 tablespoons unsalted butter
- 5 pounds elk leg (make sure silver skin and tendons are removed), cut into 2-inch cubes
- 5 large white onions, chopped
- 9 slices lean bacon, chopped
- 3 garlic cloves, finely chopped
- ½ cup sliced mushrooms, porcini if possible
- ½ cup sliced portobello mushrooms
- ½ cup sliced white button mushrooms
- 1 (750 ml) bottle full-bodied red wine, such as Burgundy
- 1 teaspoon dried sage
- 1 teaspoon sweet Hungarian paprika (or regular paprika if you do not have sweet Hungarian)
- 2 sprigs fresh thyme
- 2 dried bay leaves
- 1 tablespoon arrowroot, or 2¼ teaspoons cornstarch
- Kosher salt and freshly ground black pepper

Heat the oil and butter in a large saucepan set over high heat; add the elk and sauté, stirring occasionally, until the meat is well browned, about 5 minutes. Reduce the heat to medium and add the onions, bacon, garlic, and all the mushrooms. Sauté, stirring frequently, for about 10 minutes longer, until the vegetables and bacon have begun to brown lightly and any liquid they release has evaporated.

Transfer the elk, vegetables, and bacon to a bowl. Drain the fat from the pan and return it to medium heat. Add 2¾ cups of the wine to deglaze, stirring with a wooden spoon to loosen any browned bits on the bottom of the pan.

Return the elk, vegetables, and bacon to the pan, add the sage, paprika, thyme, and bay leaves, and bring to a boil over high heat. Reduce the heat to low, cover the pan, and simmer for about 1 hour, or until the elk is fully cooked and tender and the juices have reduced and thickened slightly.

In a small bowl, whisk together the remaining wine (about ¼ cup) and the cornstarch (or arrowroot) until velvety smooth.

Remove the thyme sprigs and bay leaves from the pan and stir the wine mixture into the ragoût in a steady stream. Simmer for about 5 minutes longer, until the ragoût has thickened, and season with salt and pepper.

CHEF'S NOTES

- Should you not have access to **elk**, any other game meat, such as venison, will do nicely. Of course, should any game meats be difficult to acquire, this dish will do nicely with pork shoulder as a substitute for the elk.

- When purchasing elk at a butcher shop or supermarket, you will have no need to further prepare the meat; all silver skin and tendons will be removed, and it will be ready to cook.

- For a great **presentation**, reserve half of the mushrooms and sauté them in butter at the last moment. Season with salt and pepper and place over the ragoût.

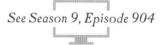

See Season 9, Episode 904

ROASTED PORK BELLY WITH CABBAGE

SERVES 6

PORK HAS BEEN A part of the American diet for so long that you may be surprised to learn that hogs are not indigenous to the Americas; the Europeans brought livestock on their ships during long voyages and this is what led to their introduction.

Many cuts of pork are popular, but one could argue that pork belly might be number one. Bacon—a beloved breakfast staple—is pork belly that has been cured and smoked. In recent years, roasted pork belly has become a fashionable American meat, often found on restaurant menus across the country.

Despite the uptick in pork belly popularity in recent years, many home cooks have never experimented with this cut. Do not be intimidated—pork belly is easy to work with, and by roasting it, you will have an experience that is much more exciting than even the best bacon.

FOR THE PORK BELLY

- 2 pounds pork belly, rind on
- Kosher salt and freshly ground black pepper
- 1 tablespoon vegetable oil

FOR THE CABBAGE

- ¼ cup lard (see Chef's Note)
- 1 medium white onion, cut into small dice
- 2 tablespoons finely chopped garlic
- 1 head savoy cabbage (2 to 2 ½ pounds)

Roast the pork belly: Preheat oven to 300°F.

With a sharp knife, make several parallel cuts across the skin and fat of the pork belly, roughly ¼ inch apart, being careful to only cut into the skin and fat, *not* the meat. Rub the pork all over with salt and pepper. Drizzle with the oil and rub in. Place the pork in a cast-iron pan or Dutch oven, skin side down.

Roast in the oven for 2 to 2½ hours, flipping the pork every ½ hour for a total of 4 turns, until the meat is tender (internal temperature of 165°F). Turn the pork belly over, skin side up. Increase the heat to 425°F and roast for about 20 minutes longer to crisp the skin. Using tongs, remove the pork from the pan and let rest for 10 minutes before slicing.

Make the cabbage: In a separate pan, melt the lard over medium heat; add the onion and garlic and sauté until translucent, 3 to 5 minutes. Cut the cabbage into quarters, remove the core, and chop cabbage into 1-inch pieces. Add the cabbage to the pan and continue to sauté, stirring occasionally, until the cabbage begins to brown slightly, 10 to 15 minutes.

Slice the pork into 1-inch chunks, using the cuts in the skin as guides, and serve over the cabbage.

CHEF'S NOTE

❧ Should you not have access to **lard**, it is never recommended to substitute butter in its place as it has a much lower smoking point and will burn. But any cooking oil will work nicely in place of lard.

See Season 9, Episode 911

➤ 147 ⬅

LAVENDER DUCK BREAST

SERVES 4

THOMAS JEFFERSON WAS FORWARD-THINKING when it came to his Monticello gardens so his approaches were often experimental. Lavender, for example, was not widely used in eighteenth-century cuisine. If *anyone* would have attempted a dish that combined duck and lavender in colonial America, an experimental gardener and epicurean like Jefferson would have been that person!

Lavender is a perfect match for duck; the rich meat of the duck just sings with the aromatic qualities of this herb, and the introduction of elderberry and coriander make it a sophisticated dish by anyone's standards. *Overnight marinating is required.*

- 4 skin-on duck breasts (4 to 5 ounces each)
- 1 teaspoon dried elderberries, crushed
- 2 tablespoons coriander, crushed
- 1 tablespoon dried lavender, crushed
- 2 tablespoons vegetable oil
- 4 ounces bacon, cut into dice
- 4 tablespoons unsalted butter
- 1 cup diced shallots
- 3 cups snow peas
- Kosher salt and freshly ground black pepper
- 1½ cups Chicken Stock (page 265 or store-bought)
- 2 cups sliced cremini mushrooms
- ½ cup red wine
- ¾ cups Demi-Glace (page 263 or store-bought)
- Chopped fresh chives, for garnish

Score the skin of the duck breasts, being careful not to cut into the meat of the duck. Rub the duck with the elderberries, coriander, and lavender, then lightly coat with the oil. Place in a glass dish, cover, and marinate in the refrigerator overnight.

Remove the duck from the marinade and pat dry with paper towels, removing excess herbs and oil to prevent burning while cooking. Place the duck breasts skin side down in a large skillet. *(Do not preheat the skillet.)* Place the skillet over medium heat and slowly render the skin until crispy and golden brown, 8 to 10 minutes. Turn the duck and sear the other side for an additional 5 to 6 minutes, until the duck reaches medium-rare (135°F internal temperature) or an additional 10 to 12 minutes for well-done (170°F). Remove from the heat and set aside to rest.

Heat a Dutch oven over medium heat. Add the bacon and cook for about 1 minute, until it begins to render its fat. Add 2 tablespoons of the butter and a ½ cup of the shallots and

sauté for 2 minutes, until the shallots are translucent, but not browned. Add the snow peas and cook, stirring, for 2 minutes. Season to taste with salt and pepper, then deglaze the pan with the stock, stirring with a wooden spoon to loosen any browned bits on the bottom of the pan. Add the sliced mushrooms and sauté for 3 to 5 minutes.

Transfer the duck breasts from the pan to a plate and return the skillet to the heat. Add the remaining ½ cup shallots and sauté until translucent. Add the red wine, stirring with a wooden spoon to loosen any browned bits on the bottom of the pan, and bring to a gentle simmer; cook until the wine is reduced by one-quarter. Add the demi-glace, return to a gentle simmer, and remove from the heat. Whisk in the remaining 2 tablespoons butter.

Slice the duck into half-inch-thick slices. Arrange the vegetables on a platter and top with sliced duck breast. Lightly drizzle the sauce over one edge of the duck and garnish with chives. Serve immediately.

CHEF'S NOTES

❧ **Duck breast** can be found at your local butcher, but should also be readily available at most grocery stores.

❧ **Elderberries** bring a distinct sweet and tart flavor to this dish and there is no substitute. Luckily, dried elderberries are stocked in most supermarkets; you should have no problem finding them in the spice aisle.

❧ **Do not preheat the skillet** prior to cooking the duck. Slowly heat it with the duck already placed in it, skin side down, to render the skin without burning it.

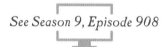

See Season 9, Episode 908

SNAPPER DORÉ

SERVES 4

WHILE FILMING THE EPISODE "Discovering Jamaica's South Coast," I had the immense pleasure of creating a meal with a local chef. This entire region is often overlooked and most travelers to the island nation of Jamaica only visit the more heavily traveled parts. This has left the South Coast of Jamaica frozen in time in certain respects; the culture has remained unaffected by outside influence and the cuisine remains historically true to form.

My experience with Jamaica is long-running and I have consulted and worked there for decades. I have traveled to just about every inch of the island and have enjoyed every town and village, but the South Coast is a place that stands alone, and as a chef and historian, it just might be my favorite region in Jamaica.

You will find this recipe to be reminiscent of classical French cuisine, but with a prominent Caribbean influence. The jerk seasoning provides a nice element of heat; you often find jerk seasoning with chicken or goat, but this blend is used in many Caribbean dishes and pairs perfectly with snapper.

- ½ cup olive oil
- Juice of 2 limes
- 4 snapper fillets, 4 to 6 ounces each
- 3 eggs, beaten
- 4 scallions, finely chopped
- 1 cup all-purpose flour
- ¼ teaspoon cayenne pepper
- Kosher salt and freshly ground white pepper
- 8 tablespoons (1 stick) unsalted butter
- ½ cup vegetable oil
- Jerk Rundown (recipe follows)

Combine the olive oil and lime juice in a shallow dish. Add the snapper fillets and marinate at room temperature for 10 to 15 minutes. Do not over-marinate or the fibers of the fish will begin to break down and the fish will turn mushy when cooked.

Meanwhile, combine the eggs with the scallions in a mixing bowl. In a separate bowl, mix the flour, cayenne, ½ teaspoon salt, and ½ teaspoon white pepper. Remove the snapper fillets from the marinade, pat dry, season with additional salt and white pepper, and then dredge them first in the seasoned flour, then in the egg.

In a large skillet, heat the butter and oil together over high heat for 1 minute, or just about to the smoking point. Place the fillets in the pan, skin side up, and cook until golden brown while continuously basting, 2 to 3 minutes. Turn fillets to skin side down and repeat basting and cooking until the fillets are golden brown, about 5 minutes longer.

Top with Jerk Rundown and serve.

JERK RUNDOWN

※ **MAKES ABOUT 1 CUP** ※

- 2 (8-ounce) cans unsweetened coconut milk
- 1 onion, diced
- 3 garlic cloves, diced
- 1 scallion, chopped
- 2 sprigs fresh thyme
- 1 habanero pepper, pierced once with a knife/fork
- 2 tablespoons jerk seasoning (see Chef's Notes)
- Kosher salt and freshly ground black pepper

Combine the coconut milk, onion, garlic, scallion, thyme, and habanero in a saucepan and bring to a boil. Immediately reduce the heat to low and continue to simmer until thick enough to coat the back of a spoon, about 20 minutes. Remove from the heat. Remove the sprig of thyme and the habanero, add the jerk seasoning, and salt and pepper to taste.

CHEF'S NOTES

- Should you wish to use another fish instead of **snapper**, feel free to do so. This recipe can be applied to many types of fish with only a single caveat: only use a firm-fleshed fish.

- When purchasing **jerk seasoning** in the store, I recommend buying a paste instead of powdered seasoning. This style, I have found, is much closer to the homemade version that you would get in the Caribbean.

- Always wear gloves when handling **habanero peppers** and be mindful to thoroughly wash your hands after using these peppers.

- For the **rundown**, only use 100 pure, unsweetened **coconut milk**.

See Season 9, Episode 903

NICARAGUAN BEEF TONGUE

SERVES 4

WHEN I FIRST MET my wife, Gloria, she knew that I was a big fan of European-style tongue recipes. I had grown up eating tongue in Germany, and the traditional Old World tongue recipes were my go-to when preparing this cut. She wanted to expand my palate and show me how tongue is prepared in her home country of Nicaragua.

I remember watching her make this dish and waited in great anticipation; she was using completely different spices and methods than I was accustomed to and I did not know what to expect. Not only was I impressed with this recipe, but I also enjoyed it so much that it has been a regular feature on our dinner table for the past forty years!

When I traveled with my film crew to Nicaragua for an episode, I was able to capture this method on film. This recipe is deeply personal to me, but it is not just a wistful nostalgia that inspires me; the incredible flavor and texture is sure to move you as well.

FOR THE BEEF TONGUE

- 2 whole cloves
- 2 bay leaves
- 1 large white onion, cut in half
- 1 whole beef tongue (3 to 3½ pounds)
- 2 tablespoons pickling spice

FOR THE SAUCE

- 3 tablespoons unsalted butter
- 2 large white onions, coarsely chopped
- 2 green bell peppers, cut into ¼-inch strips
- ½ cup white rum
- ½ cup cola
- ¼ cup Worcestershire sauce
- 2 tablespoons petite capers
- 2 tablespoons raisins
- ¼ cup tomato ketchup
- Kosher salt and freshly ground black pepper

Make the tongue: Use a clove to tack a bay leaf to each onion half to make the onion piquet.

In a large pot of salted water, add the onion piquet, beef tongue, and pickling spice and bring to a rolling boil over high heat. Simmer until the tongue is firm, about 1½ hours, periodically skimming off any impurities that rise to the top and adding water throughout the process to keep the tongue fully submerged. Reduce the heat to a medium boil and continue cooking for 30 minutes longer, until the tongue is tender.

Remove from the heat and let the tongue cool in the stock, making sure that it remains completely covered. Once the tongue is cool, peel off the skin and trim off any excess fat. Slice on a bias into 8 slices about ¾ inch thick. The tongue may be kept refrigerated until you are ready to assemble the dish.

Make the sauce: In a large sauté pan, melt the butter over medium heat. Add the chopped onions and cook, stirring occasionally with a wooden spoon, until they begin to wilt and become translucent but not browned. Add the green peppers and continue to cook for 3 to 4 minutes. Add the tongue slices, rum, cola, and Worcestershire sauce and simmer for 5 to 10 minutes. Add the capers, raisins, and ketchup, adjust seasoning with salt and pepper if necessary, and simmer for 3 to 5 minutes.

Use tongs to place the tongue on a platter, top with sauce, and serve immediately.

CHEF'S NOTES

- For the best results, allow the **tongue** to completely cool before slicing.

- Only use **white onions** in this recipe. Other varieties will not produce the desired flavor profile.

- **Mexican Coca-Cola** will provide the most authentic flavor. It can be found at most beverage retailers.

See Season 9, Episode 912

5

SIDE DISHES

Seasonal Accompaniments to the Main Course

*I*n eighteenth-century America, the custom was to serve meals family style. A large platter with the meat and vegetables and sauce (if there was one), was placed in the center of the table and everyone would help themselves to what they wanted.

Nowadays, we tend to think of a meal in parts; the main course is a separate item from side dishes of vegetables and grains. Here, you'll find recipes for delectable sides that complement a main course. While gathering side dishes into their own chapter isn't fully historically accurate, I hope it will give you a bit more flexibility in choosing the layout of your own family meal.

There is something here to go with every meat and seafood menu. From hearty dishes like Cauliflower and Potato Casserole, to delicate preparations like Peas à la Française, the recipes here provide you with twelve months' worth of delicious, crowd-pleasing seasonal dishes.

Bouillon Potatoes

Stewed Mushrooms

Fennel Puree

Braised Sunchokes

Peas à la Française

Potato Broccoli Casserole

Fried Celery

Almond Rice Pilaf

Cauliflower and Potato Casserole

Pumpkin Pancakes

Potato Croquettes

Creamed Kohlrabi

Sautéed Heirloom Carrots

Stewed Leeks with Irish Bacon

Honey-Stung Brussels Sprouts

Potato Gratin

Mashed Potatoes with Fried Horseradish

Ragoût of Salsify and Cardoon

Chestnut Rice Pilaf

Sautéed Swiss Chard

BOUILLON POTATOES

THIS RECIPE USES THE beef broth created in the Bouilli (Boiled Beef) recipe on page 85, elevating the humble potato from a simple accompaniment to a truly flavorful dish. Thomas Jefferson would have enjoyed this side dish often, as one of his favorite meals was bouilli, which is traditionally paired with these potatoes. In fact, the dish is thought to have been served at Monticello several times a month during Jefferson's life at the estate, the chefs gathering all the needed potatoes, vegetables, and herbs directly from the gardens.

- ❦ 2 tablespoons vegetable oil
- ❦ 1 white onion, cut into ½-inch dice
- ❦ 1 carrot, peeled and cut into ½-inch dice
- ❦ 1 turnip, peeled and cut into ½-inch dice
- ❦ 1 stalk celery, cut into ½-inch dice
- ❦ 1 leek, cleaned and cut into ½-inch strips
- ❦ 2 garlic cloves, minced
- ❦ 8 to 10 Irish white or Yukon Gold potatoes, cut into ½-inch dice (10 cups)
- ❦ 5 to 8 cups beef broth from Bouilli (page 85), or see Chef's Note
- ❦ 1 bay leaf
- ❦ 2 sprigs fresh thyme, optional

Heat the oil in a large sauté pan over medium heat. Add the onion, carrot, turnip, celery, and leek and cook for 2 minutes. Add the garlic and sauté until translucent but not browned. Increase the heat to high and continue to sauté the vegetables, stirring with a wooden spoon to prevent burning, for about 2 minutes.

Add the potatoes and enough broth to just cover them. Add the bay leaf and the thyme sprigs if using. Bring just to a boil then reduce to a simmer and cook for about 15 minutes, or until the potatoes are fork tender. Remove the bay leaf and thyme, transfer the potatoes to a serving dish, top the potatoes with a little of the cooking liquid, and serve immediately.

CHEF'S NOTE

- ❦ If you are not making the Bouilli (Boiled Beef), the **beef stock** on page 264 or even store-bought beef stock will work well in this recipe.
- ❦ This side dish is traditionally paired with Bouilli, but this savory potatoes side can be a **perfect accompaniment** to many other meats and even seafood. Feel free to experiment with this versatile recipe!

See Season 1, Episode 106

STEWED MUSHROOMS

SERVES 4

"Gather grown mushrooms, but such as are young enough to have red gills; cut off that part of the stem which grew in the earth, wash them carefully and take the skin from the top; put them into a stew-pan with some salt, but no water, stew them till tender, and thicken them with a spoonful of butter mixed with one of brown flour; red wine may be added, but the flavor of the mushroom is too delicious to require aid from anything." So wrote Mary Randolph in the 1824 edition of her classic cookbook, *The Virginia Housewife*.

This is a simple recipe that is sure to impress. Unlike other recipes found within this book, this one comes directly from the pages of history. Sometimes, you cannot add to perfection! The recipe is also very dear to my heart: my very first Emmy came from this episode!

- 3 tablespoons unsalted butter, at room temperature
- 4 cups button mushrooms with stems, cleaned
- 1½ teaspoons kosher salt
- 1½ cups dry red wine, such as Burgundy
- 2 tablespoons brown flour (see Chef's Note)
- 1 tablespoon finely chopped fresh parsley
- Freshly ground black pepper

In a sauté pan over high heat, melt 1 tablespoon of the butter. Add the mushrooms and sprinkle with the salt. Cook over high heat, stirring constantly, until the mushrooms wilt, about 3 minutes. Add the wine and bring just to a boil. Lower the heat to a simmer and continue cooking until the liquid is reduced by half, about 5 minutes.

In a small bowl, mix the remaining 2 tablespoons butter with the brown flour. Add the flour-butter mixture to the pan 1 teaspoon at a time, whisking for about 5 minutes, until the liquid becomes creamy and the mushrooms are tender.

Add the parsley and the black pepper to taste and serve hot.

--- CHEF'S NOTE ---

- **Brown flour** is actually *baked* all-purpose flour. It may be available in specialty food stores in some areas, but if it is not available, it is easy to make your own: Place all-purpose flour on a baking sheet and bake in a 375°F oven for about 8 to 10 minutes. Keep a close eye; when the flour is a golden brown, remove and allow to cool before use.

See Season 1, Episode 108

FENNEL PUREE

SERVES 8

FENNEL IS FOUND THROUGHOUT this cookbook and throughout history for a good reason; it grows very well in a wide variety of climates and soils and is considered a hardy plant.

- ❦ 5 large fresh fennel bulbs, leaves chopped and reserved, with a few whole sprigs, for garnish
- ❦ 2 medium round red potatoes (about 4 ounces), peeled and sliced
- ❦ 3 tablespoons heavy cream
- ❦ Kosher salt and freshly ground black pepper
- ❦ ½ cup grated Parmesan cheese, for serving
- ❦ 1 tablespoon sweet paprika, for serving

Season 2, Episode 201

Cut off the bases, tops, and any bruised or tough outer layers of the fennel. Cut each fennel bulb into 6 pieces and remove the core.

In a large saucepan, cover the fennel and potatoes with lightly salted water and bring to a boil over high heat. Reduce heat to medium and cook for 15 to 20 minutes, until the vegetables are fork tender. Drain and cool slightly.

Transfer the vegetables to a blender or food processor and puree until smooth. Add the cream and process until combined. Season with salt and pepper to taste.

Transfer to a serving bowl. Sprinkle the Parmesan and paprika over the puree and garnish with 1 tablespoon of the chopped fennel leaves and a few whole sprigs. Serve hot.

BRAISED SUNCHOKES

SERVES 8

WITH WINTER'S LIMITED SUPPLY of fruits and vegetables, colonial cooks looked to root vegetables, sunchokes, and cabbages for side dishes. They were cooked in braises and stews and roasted to accompany meats and other main courses.

The sunchoke is an interesting ingredient: it is the knobby root of the sunflower, with an appearance similar to fresh ginger root and a flavor like the heart of an artichoke. It was one of the first culinary introductions from the Native Americans to the colonists in the early days of American history. Sunchokes are widely available and often sold under the name Jerusalem artichoke.

- 2 tablespoons olive oil
- 8 ounces bacon, diced
- 1 medium white onion, chopped
- 2 cups chopped chanterelle mushrooms
- 8 large fresh sunchokes, peeled and chopped
- Juice of 1 lemon
- Kosher salt and freshly ground white pepper

Preheat oven to 375°F.

Pour the olive oil into a Dutch oven and add, in layers, the bacon, onion, and chanterelles. Add the sunchokes and squeeze the juice of a lemon over them. Generously season with salt and pepper. Bake covered tightly with foil for 20 minutes, or until the sunchokes are tender but not overcooked. Serve hot.

See Season 3, Episode 302

PEAS À LA FRANÇAISE

SERVES 6 TO 8

FRENCH CUISINE WAS EN vogue in colonial America and known to be one of Thomas Jefferson's favorites. He wrote in letters that peas were among his most prized plants—he planted twenty-eight varieties at Monticello—and a favorite spring crop. There could be very few side dishes that are more representative of Jefferson than this one.

- 7 tablespoons unsalted butter, at room temperature
- 3 tablespoons all-purpose flour
- 3 cups pearl onions, peeled
- ¼ cup water
- 4 cups shelled fresh peas
- 2 cups heavy cream
- ½ teaspoon fresh thyme leaves
- 1 teaspoon kosher salt
- ¼ teaspoon freshly ground black pepper
- 1 head romaine lettuce, finely chopped

Knead together the butter and flour to form a *beurre manié*, using your hands or, if you prefer, a fork.

In a large saucepan, melt 4 tablespoons of the *beurre manié* over medium heat; add the onions and sauté until translucent, 3 to 5 minutes. Add the water and peas, cover the pan, and cook for about 5 minutes, or until the peas are tender. Add the cream, thyme, salt, and pepper. Stir in the remaining *beurre manié* and allow the sauce to thicken slightly.

Just before serving, add the lettuce to the peas, toss gently, and leave over heat just until the lettuce is wilted. Serve immediately.

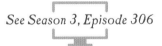
See Season 3, Episode 306

POTATO BROCCOLI CASSEROLE

SERVES 6 TO 8

AS WINTER APPROACHED AND the availability of fresh vegetables began to wane, colonial cooks would hide inferior vegetables in casseroles, stews, ragoûts, and puddings. But you won't find this recipe to be "inferior" in any way!

FOR THE CASSEROLE

- 4 tablespoons unsalted butter, softened
- 1 tablespoon minced garlic
- ¼ cup all-purpose flour
- 2 cups whole milk
- 2 cups shredded Cheddar cheese
- 1 large head broccoli, blanched (see Chef's Notes) and chopped
- 8 to 10 large russet potatoes, peeled, sliced, and blanched (see Chef's Notes)

FOR THE TOPPING

- 2 tablespoons unsalted butter, melted
- 1½ cups fresh bread crumbs
- ¼ cup shredded Cheddar cheese
- ½ teaspoon kosher salt

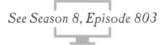

See Season 8, Episode 803

Preheat oven to 350°F.

To make the casserole: In a large bowl, combine all of the casserole ingredients. Place the mixture in a 9 by 13-inch baking dish.

To make the topping: Combine the topping ingredients and distribute evenly over the casserole.

Bake for 30 to 35 minutes, until the topping is golden brown and the casserole is bubbling hot.

CHEF'S NOTES

- Should you not wish to chop a whole head of **broccoli**, I recommend purchasing the 1-pound package of pre-chopped florets available in every supermarket.

- To properly **blanch** the potatoes and broccoli, use separate pots, or blanch separately, as the blanch times vary greatly. Bring water to boil in a medium stockpot. Add the potatoes and cook for about 10 minutes, until barely tender; then remove from heat. The same process goes for the broccoli, but the blanching time is only about 4 minutes.

FRIED CELERY

SERVES 6

CRUNCHY, RAW CELERY IS a popular snack today, but it would not have been served in the eighteenth century. Fried celery may sound odd, but it is a delish and delightfully different way to enjoy this vegetable, especially during the winter.

- 1 bunch celery, trimmed, cut into stalks
- 2¼ cups all-purpose flour
- 3 eggs, beaten
- 1¼ cups whole milk
- 1½ tablespoons clarified butter (see Chef's Notes, page 17) or olive oil
- ⅛ teaspoon freshly grated nutmeg
- ⅛ teaspoon kosher salt
- ⅛ teaspoon freshly ground white pepper
- 4 cups vegetable oil, for frying

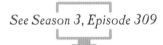
See Season 3, Episode 309

In a large saucepan, bring 2 quarts of lightly salted water to a boil over high heat. Add the celery and cook until just tender, 2 to 3 minutes. Drain and return the celery to the pan.

Add enough cold water to cover the celery completely and let stand for about 5 minutes, until the celery is cool. Drain again and pat dry with paper towel.

In a large mixing bowl, whisk together the flour, eggs, milk, clarified butter, nutmeg, salt, and pepper to create a batter.

Heat the oil to 350°F in a deep-fat fryer or 4-quart heavy saucepan over high heat.

A few stalks at a time, dip the celery in the batter, shaking off any excess, then carefully drop into the heated oil. Fry until golden brown, 3 to 4 minutes. Using a slotted spoon, remove the celery from the oil and place on a baking sheet lined with paper towels to absorb any excess oil. Serve hot.

ALMOND RICE PILAF

SERVES 6 TO 8

IN COLONIAL TIMES, RICE was an export crop grown in the wetlands of South Carolina and Georgia and sold in the European markets through English brokers. While minister to France, Jefferson pondered the tepid sales of American rice, believing that it didn't sell well because of inferior quality. When he embarked on his tour of the major wine-producing regions in France, he made a side trip to Italy to smuggle, under penalty of death, some rice grains out of Piedmont. He recounted that "I could only bring off as much as my coat and surtout pockets could hold." He hoped that sowing this strain of rice in America would boost sales in France. Not long after this harrowing exercise, he learned that poor sales were the result of high prices, rather than poor quality, so upon his return to America, he arranged to take the English middlemen out of the equation and sell rice directly to France.

- 2 tablespoons unsalted butter
- 2 tablespoons vegetable oil
- 1 medium onion, finely diced
- 2 cups long-grain rice
- 1 cup almonds, crushed
- 3 cups Chicken Stock (page 265 or store-bought)
- 1 bay leaf
- Kosher salt and freshly ground black pepper
- 1 tablespoon chopped fresh parsley
- 1 cup sliced almonds, toasted

Preheat oven to 400°F.

Melt 1 tablespoon of the butter in the vegetable oil in large sauté pan over medium heat. Add the onion and cook for 3 to 5 minutes, until translucent. Add the rice and cook for 2 minutes, until toasted. Transfer to a deep ovenproof dish and stir in the remaining 1 tablespoon butter, crushed almonds, stock, and bay leaf. Cover and bake for 40 minutes, or until the rice is cooked.

Fluff the rice with a fork, remove the bay leaf, and season with salt and pepper. Sprinkle the parsley and sliced almonds over the rice, toss gently, and serve hot.

See Season 3, Episode 311

CAULIFLOWER AND POTATO CASSEROLE

SERVES 10 TO 12

HISTORICALLY, HEARTY SIDE DISHES were served in copious amounts at City Tavern feasts. It wasn't uncommon to have as many as ten served in one meal, including vegetables of all types, barley, rice, potatoes, and stuffing. This dish may have been on the table among many other savory sides. Potato and cauliflower work exceptionally well together, similar in color, but incredibly different in flavor and texture.

- 10 to 12 small Yukon Gold potatoes, peeled
- Kosher salt
- 1 large head cauliflower, cut into florets
- 3 tablespoons unsalted butter, at room temperature
- ½ cup sour cream
- ½ cup milk
- 1 cup shredded Cheddar cheese
- Freshly ground white pepper
- ¼ cup crumbs from Sally Lunn Bread (page 194)
- 1 teaspoon sweet Hungarian paprika (or regular paprika)

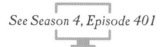
See Season 4, Episode 401

Preheat oven to 350°F. Butter a large baking dish or casserole

Place the potatoes in a large saucepan and cover with cold water. Season lightly with salt and bring just to a boil over high heat. Reduce the heat to medium and simmer until just fork tender, 10 to 15 minutes.

Meanwhile, bring a large saucepan of lightly salted water to a boil over high heat. Add the cauliflower and boil until the florets are very soft, about 10 minutes.

Drain the potatoes and cauliflower and combine them in a large bowl. Add the butter, sour cream, milk, and cheese and mash until smooth. Season with salt and pepper to taste.

Pour into the buttered baking dish and sprinkle evenly with the bread crumbs and paprika. Bake until golden brown and bubbly, about 30 minutes. Serve hot.

CHEF'S NOTE

- Should your local supermarket or spice shop not carry **sweet Hungarian paprika,** this recipe will work very nicely with the standard paprika.

PUMPKIN PANCAKES

 SERVES 6 TO 8

PUMPKIN, NATIVE TO THE Caribbean, became very popular in the British and American colonies as it lasted for a long time on ships and was often imported into port cities. This unique Caribbean side dish is often served with spicy curry dishes; the rich flavor of pumpkin pairs perfectly with curried seafood, and the sweetness helps cool off some of the intense heat that you find in island cooking.

This recipe is an unusual one in that it requires fresh pumpkin. Canned or frozen alternatives will work as substitutes in many pumpkin recipes, but this is not one of them. Although there is a little more effort needed with cutting the fresh pumpkin, the end result is spectacular! Try to find pie pumpkins or even heirloom varieties, which are more like those native to the islands.

- 1 small to medium pumpkin or butternut squash, peeled, seeded, and cut into six pieces
- 4 cups all-purpose flour
- 1 (12-ounce) can evaporated milk
- 2 teaspoons vanilla extract
- 1 teaspoon freshly grated nutmeg
- ¼ teaspoon kosher salt
- 1 teaspoon sugar, to taste
- Vegetable oil, for frying

See Season 4, Episode 404

Grate the pumpkin flesh into a bowl and then add the flour, evaporated milk, vanilla, nutmeg, salt, and sugar. (Add as much sugar as you prefer, more to make sweeter dessert-like pancakes or less for savory pancakes.) Mix everything together to make a batter with cake-like consistency.

Pour enough oil into a frying pan to cover the bottom, and set the pan over medium heat. When the oil is hot but not smoking, ladle small portions (about 3 tablespoons) of the batter into the pan and fry until light brown in color on both sides, 2 to 3 minutes per side. Cook in batches; keep warm in oven while finishing.

POTATO CROQUETTES

SERVES 8

MANY COOKS LIKE TO use this recipe as a way of reusing last night's mashed potatoes. Colonial cooks may have served croquettes for breakfast or as the small meal that ended the day, rather than with the major meal, which was served midday.

- ❦ 8 large Yukon Gold potatoes, peeled and cut into 1-inch cubes
- ❦ 4 egg yolks, beaten
- ❦ 1 teaspoon kosher salt
- ❦ ½ teaspoon freshly ground white pepper
- ❦ ⅛ teaspoon freshly grated nutmeg
- ❦ 1 quart vegetable oil
- ❦ 2 cups fresh bread crumbs

Preheat oven to 300°F.

Place potatoes in a large saucepan and cover with cold water. Season lightly with salt and bring just to a boil over high heat. Reduce the heat to medium and simmer until fork tender, 10 to 15 minutes.

Drain the potatoes, place on a baking sheet, and set in the warm oven to dry further, about 5 minutes. Then, set them aside to cool slightly.

Put the potatoes through a potato ricer or food mill into a large bowl; add the egg yolks, salt, pepper, and nutmeg and mix thoroughly to combine.

Pour the oil into a large, high-sided pan and heat to 350°F over medium heat.

Place the bread crumbs on a plate. Using slightly wet hands, shape the potatoes into balls about 1½ inches in diameter, then roll in the bread crumbs until coated.

In batches and without overcrowding the pan, gently place the potato croquettes in the hot oil and fry until golden brown, 2 to 3 minutes, turning midway through the cooking time. Carefully remove with a slotted spoon and place on a plate lined with paper towels to absorb any excess oil. Serve immediately.

See Season 4, Episode 409

CREAMED KOHLRABI

SERVES 4 TO 6

KOHLRABI MAY SEEM LIKE an exotic ingredient to today's cooks, but eighteenth-century gardens were filled with a variety of vegetables in all growing seasons. This crunchy root vegetable would have been served in the cooler months when gardeners could pluck one from the ground just before frost.

Kohlrabi can truly be considered a Pan-European ingredient. It is used commonly throughout most regions in Europe. This made the transition to the New World an obvious one, and it was planted in many eighteenth-century gardens in the colonies. The recipe is from an episode featuring our fifth president, James Monroe, who always had kohlrabi in his personal gardens.

- 1 pound kohlrabies, the smaller the better (see Chef's Notes)
- 2 tablespoons vegetable oil
- Béchamel Sauce (page 248)
- ½ teaspoon freshly grated nutmeg

Trim the greens and tops of the kohlrabies, julienne them, and set aside. Peel and cut the kohlrabi bulbs in half, then slice in half-moon shapes. In a medium saucepan, bring salted water to a boil over high heat. Blanch the bulb slices until al dente, 3 to 4 minutes, and set aside.

Heat the oil in a skillet over medium-high heat until hot but not smoking. Add the kohlrabi greens to the oil and fry until crisp, about 2 minutes, being careful not to burn them.

Arrange the blanched kohlrabi on a platter, cover with warm béchamel and top with the fried kohlrabi greens. Sprinkle the dish with fresh nutmeg and serve immediately.

CHEF'S NOTES

- When purchasing kohlrabies, it is important to pick the youngest available. The perfect size of a **young kohlrabi** is approximately the size of a small fist; the larger kohlrabies tend to be more fibrous and do not work as well in this recipe.

- Be careful when frying the **kohlrabi greens**; although it is a tough vegetable and is somewhat forgiving, the greens can burn easily.

See Season 4, Episode 410

SAUTÉED HEIRLOOM CARROTS

 SERVES 4

CARROTS ARE ONE OF the most common vegetables in the world; they are enjoyed raw, or can be cooked in an endless number of ways. It may come as a surprise that their signature bright orange color is an example of early genetic engineering. Carrots were naturally purple, white, or yellow, and it was not until the seventeenth century that carrots were bred to be orange in honor of William of Orange, the soldier and politician who helped establish the Netherlands as an independent state in the 1500s.

While the orange color has remained the standard hue for carrots ever since, there are colorful heirloom carrots available in many gourmet supermarkets and farmers' markets across the country.

- 1 pound heirloom carrots (8 to 10 carrots)
- 3 tablespoons unsalted butter
- 3 medium shallots, diced
- Freshly ground black pepper
- Chopped fresh parsley, for garnish

See Season 5, Episode 511

Wash and scrape the carrots. (Do not peel the carrots with a peeler, just give them a quick, rough scraping with a fork or rub with a clean towel.) Cut the carrots on a bias into approximately 1-inch bites.

In a sauté pan, melt the butter over medium heat. Add the shallots and cook until just translucent, 3 to 4 minutes. Increase the heat to medium-high, add the carrots, and cook, stirring frequently, until just al dente, 7 to 10 minutes.

Season with pepper to taste and garnish with parsley.

STEWED LEEKS with IRISH BACON

SERVES 6 TO 8

THIS SIMPLE RECIPE ALLOWS leeks to take on the rich flavors of two kinds of bacon. The leeks are a bit sweet and the bacon a bit salty, so it's a great combination in this colorful, spring-green side dish that's sure to please.

Bacon was used often in the eighteenth century and the majority of homes would have a slab of bacon hanging in their larder or root cellar. Should you not wish to use Irish bacon (aka Canadian bacon) specifically, any bacon will work nicely. If you do not have lard or schmaltz, any cooking oil will do fine in its place.

- ♥ 2 tablespoons lard or schmaltz (see Chef's Note, page 38) (or vegetable oil)
- ♥ 4 garlic cloves, coarsely chopped
- ♥ 4 small onions, coarsely chopped
- ♥ 8 leeks, white and light green parts only, washed and cut into 2-inch pieces
- ♥ 2 cups Vegetable Stock (page 268 or store-bought), warmed
- ♥ 8 ounces smoked bacon, chopped
- ♥ 8 ounces Irish (Canadian) bacon, chopped
- ♥ 3 sprigs fresh thyme, for garnish

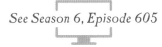

See Season 6, Episode 605

Cook the lard (or schmaltz or oil), garlic, and onions in a saucepan set over medium heat for 3 to 5 minutes, stirring occasionally with a wooden spoon, until the onions are translucent but not browned. Add the leeks and stock and stir to combine. Add the bacon. Cover the pan with a lid and let simmer for about 10 minutes, until the liquid is almost entirely evaporated.

Place the stewed leeks and bacon in a serving dish and garnish with fresh thyme. Serve immediately.

CHEF'S NOTE

- ♥ Due to the many-layered structure of **leeks**, they are very good at hiding the sandy material they are grown in. Give extra attention to the cleaning of the leeks to ensure that all sand and soil is removed before cooking.

HONEY-STUNG BRUSSELS SPROUTS

SERVES 6 TO 8

BRUSSELS SPROUTS ARE MY favorite vegetable, a nod to my German heritage, so I was very pleased when the chefs at the Omni Homestead suggested this recipe to cook on an episode of *A Taste of History*. It is a favorite at the Omni Homestead and was probably just as popular when, in 1818, Thomas Jefferson spent three weeks at the hot springs for their therapeutic value. The springs are said to cure a wide variety of ailments; certainly, the heat and mineral content soothes arthritis and sore muscles. (Filming the show is an intense process and I was happy for the chance to try them out myself.)

In recent years, Brussels sprouts have become a common dish at restaurants across the country. This once overlooked member of the cabbage family is coming into the spotlight.

- 8 ounces slab bacon, cut into lardons (see Chef's Notes)
- Vegetable oil, for frying
- 1½ pounds Brussels sprouts, cut into quarters
- ¼ cup honey
- 4 ounces farmstead (or Gruyère) cheese, shaved
- Kosher salt and freshly ground black pepper

In a sauté pan, fry the bacon over medium-high heat until crispy, 5 to 7 minutes. Transfer the bacon to a sheet lined with paper towels and set aside.

Add oil to a Dutch oven or large deep skillet to a depth of 1 inch and set over medium-high heat. When the oil reaches 350°F, add the Brussels sprouts and cook until golden brown and crispy, 2 to 3 minutes. Transfer the sprouts to a serving bowl and toss with the crisp bacon, honey, cheese, and salt and pepper to taste. Serve warm.

CHEF'S NOTES

- While bacon normally comes pre-sliced in packages, the meat section of your supermarket will also have unsliced or **slab bacon**. This is essential to this recipe, as lardons cannot be made with sliced bacon.

- **Lardons** are a staple in French cuisine and very easy to cut at home! Take the slab bacon and slice into ⅛-inch matchsticks. (If you enjoy the process of preparing lardons at home, they can be incorporated into any dish that calls for bacon.)

See Season 6, Episode 606

POTATO GRATIN

THIS RECIPE IS ONE that has stood the test of time—almost everyone has made a potato gratin at some point. This elegant version is befitting our episode that focused on *L'Hermione*—the ship that carried General Lafayette to the colonies, where he joined forces with George Washington and, thus, changed the course of history. The recipe would have been prepared in the ship's galley while en route to America. Potatoes were common during transoceanic voyages, but the addition of Gruyère cheese changes the dish from simple to extravagant.

- 8 large baking potatoes, peeled and thinly sliced
- Freshly ground white pepper
- Kosher salt
- Pinch nutmeg
- 1 cup Chicken Stock (page 265 or store-bought)
- ½ cup dry white wine
- 2 tablespoons olive oil
- 1 cup shredded Gruyère cheese
- Chopped fresh parsley, for garnish

Preheat oven to 375°F.

Layer the potatoes in a large baking dish, shingling them on top of each other slightly and seasoning each layer lightly with white pepper and salt. Sprinkle with nutmeg. Ladle the stock over potatoes, followed by the wine. Drizzle with the olive oil and top with the cheese.

Bake the gratin for about 25 minutes, until the cheese is browned and the potatoes are fork tender and cooked through. Garnish with fresh parsley and serve immediately.

See Season 6, Episode 610

MASHED POTATOES WITH FRIED HORSERADISH

SERVES 6 TO 8

SINCE IT IS A member of the lethal nightshade family, the potato was long considered by Europeans to be poisonous. The leaves are indeed poisonous, but the potato itself, lacking exposure to the sun, never has the chance to activate its latent poisonous quality. As with the tomato—which was thought to be unfit for human consumption until Thomas Jefferson became its champion and forced his friends to eat it—the potato initially encountered a great deal of resistance. In the sixteenth century, Sir Walter Raleigh effectively made the case for potatoes in England by planting them on lands he owned in Ireland. Two centuries later, in the 1780s, people on the Continent still weren't convinced, until Antoine-Augustin Parmentier brought potatoes into vogue in France by convincing King Louis XVI and Marie Antoinette to try them and serve them at court. Various forms of this most basic recipe for potatoes have existed since that time.

- 1½ pounds Yukon Gold potatoes, peeled and cut into 1-inch cubes
- 4 tablespoons unsalted butter
- ¼ cup heavy cream
- ½ teaspoon freshly grated nutmeg
- Kosher salt and freshly ground black pepper
- Fried Horseradish Garnish (recipe follows)

In a large saucepan or stockpot, combine the potatoes with just enough salted water to cover and bring to a boil over high heat. Reduce the heat and simmer for 15 to 20 minutes, until the potatoes are fork tender. Drain the potatoes and return them to the saucepan, allowing the steam to escape so the potatoes dry.

Add the butter and cream and mash with a potato masher until smooth. Season with the nutmeg and salt and pepper to taste. Garnish with fried horseradish.

FRIED HORSERADISH GARNISH

❋ MAKES ABOUT 1 CUP ❋

HORSERADISH, LIKE BRUSSELS SPROUTS, would have been left in the garden all winter, then harvested and fried in lard to enhance drab winter dishes.

❦ 1 (3-inch) piece fresh horseradish root, peeled

❦ 1 cup vegetable oil, for frying

See Season 7, Episode 703

Julienne the horseradish as finely as possible. Thoroughly pat dry between paper towels.

Pour the oil into a medium saucepan and heat over medium heat to 350°F. Carefully add the horseradish, in batches if needed, and cook until golden brown, 2 to 3 minutes. Be careful not to let the horseradish burn. Using a slotted spoon, remove the horseradish and place on a paper towel to drain excess oil.

CHEF'S NOTE

❦ Every spice begins to lose its flavor as soon as it is ground, and nothing can compare to the flavor that freshly ground **nutmeg** imparts to a dish. Whole nutmeg is available in virtually every supermarket and spice store nowadays.

RAGOÛT OF SALSIFY AND CARDOON

SERVES 4 TO 6

BELIEVED TO HAVE BEEN brought to America by Europeans, salsify—a root vegetable that resembles a slender parsnip—became a favorite of the colonists because it wintered well in root cellars. Its subtle, oyster-like flavor lent itself to many preparations and paired well with almost any meat, fowl, or fish.

The cardoon is an equally exotic ingredient: also known as a globe artichoke, this vegetable is native to the Mediterranean region of Europe and North Africa. It produces beautiful violet flowers and its flavor is reminiscent of a more complex artichoke.

- 2 tablespoons unsalted butter
- 4 black salsify, peeled, cut into 2-inch pieces and kept in water with lemon to prevent browning
- 1 large (14-ounce) head cardoon, washed, trimmed, and cut into ½-inch half-moons
- ¼ cup finely chopped shallots
- ¼ cup whiskey
- Juice of 1 lemon
- 2 cups heavy cream
- 1½ cups Demi-Glace (page 263 or store-bought)
- ¼ cup chopped fresh parsley
- Kosher salt and freshly ground black pepper

Melt the butter in a large skillet over high heat. Drain the salsify of its lemon water and add to skillet, along with the cardoon and shallots. Sauté for 5 to 6 minutes.

Add the whiskey to the pan, wait 30 to 60 seconds, then carefully light it with a match to flambé. When the flames die down, add the lemon juice and reduce until almost all liquid has cooked off. Add the cream and continue to cook until reduced by half. Add the demi-glace and parsley. Stir and season with salt and pepper to taste. Serve immediately.

CHEF'S NOTES

- For those who do not have experience with **flambé,** it is a great way to quickly infuse the flavors of a spirit into your dish. Alcohol burns very quickly, and after a flash of flame, you will have the rich whiskey flavor without the alcohol content.

- After pouring the **whiskey** into the pan, it is important to allow it to heat until bubbling prior to lighting. This will take less than 1 minute.

- This recipe calls for a **match** to be used to ignite the whiskey, but it is perfectly fine to use a **long-handled kitchen lighter**.

See Season 8, Episode 801

CHESTNUT RICE PILAF

SERVES 6

CHESTNUT TREES DOTTED THE Eastern Seaboard in colonial times, dropping their fruit for anyone who could brave the spiny outer coating and hard inner shell to get to the delectable nut meat inside. As far back as 1636, it was noted that the American chestnut was "sweeter and generally superior" to European chestnuts.

- ⍦ 3 tablespoons unsalted butter
- ⍦ 1 small onion, cut into small dice
- ⍦ 1 tablespoon chopped garlic
- ⍦ 3 cups converted white rice
- ⍦ 12 roasted chestnuts, coarsely chopped
- ⍦ 4 cups cold Chicken Stock (page 265 or store-bought)
- ⍦ ¼ cup chopped fresh parsley
- ⍦ Kosher salt and freshly ground black pepper

In a large saucepan, melt the butter over medium heat. Add the onion and garlic and cook over low heat for 2 minutes, until translucent but not browned. Add the rice, chestnuts, and stock and bring just to a boil. Reduce to a simmer and cook for 20 minutes, or until the rice is cooked and no liquid remains.

Gently fold in the parsley, season with salt and pepper, and serve.

CHEF'S NOTES

- ⍦ **Chestnuts** are available pre-roasted and chopped in most Asian supermarkets. If you are a purist like me, take the extra step to roast them yourself.

- ⍦ **To roast chestnuts:** Wash and dry the chestnuts then lightly score the top of each with an X. Place the chestnuts, equally spaced, on a baking sheet and bake at 425°F until the skin begins to pull away from the scores, 20 to 30 minutes. Allow to cool before chopping.

See Season 8, Episode 807

SAUTÉED SWISS CHARD

SERVES 4

THOMAS JEFFERSON GREW SWISS chard in his garden under the names "white beet" or "spinach beet," and used the tender young plants in salads. His chef also steamed the mature leaves and used the center rib in stews, similar to how we use celery today.

- 2 tablespoons lard or schmaltz (see Chef's Note, page 38) (or vegetable oil)
- 8 ounces bacon, chopped
- 1 medium onion, diced small
- 1 tablespoon chopped garlic (about 2 cloves)
- 2 bunches Swiss chard, rinsed well and cut into 2-inch pieces
- Kosher salt and fresh ground black pepper

In a large skillet set over medium heat, cook the lard (or schmaltz or oil) and bacon until the bacon is crisp, about 4 minutes. Add the onion and garlic and cook for 2 minutes, or until the onion is translucent. Add the Swiss chard, toss, and cook an additional 4 to 5 minutes, until the chard is tender. Season with salt and pepper and serve immediately.

See Season 8, Episode 810

6

BREADS

Sweet and Savory, Yeasted and Quick—
Loaves, Rolls, and Fritters

read was a staple at every meal in eighteenth-century America and it was, of course, homemade. Unlike today, when most of us rely on supermarkets for loaves of sliced bread or bags of English muffins, every young girl (except those raised in wealthy households) learned how to make yeasted and un-yeasted breads, rolls, biscuits, and scones.

Breads were baked in a beehive oven integrated into a wall adjacent to the kitchen's open hearth or, if there was no wall oven, directly over the coals of an open fire. The dough was cooked in a cast-iron skillet or spider (a cast-iron skillet with three legs to hold it up off the coals), or Dutch oven, muffin pans, beautifully shaped Bundt-like pans, or on a cast-iron griddle. From a young age, women mastered the ins and outs of working with yeast, and learned how to gauge the

temperature of the oven or coals so as not to burn the bread.

Wheat flour was a more expensive commodity than cornmeal in those days, so the colonists adapted their European recipes accordingly. And, like all foods that passed through an eighteenth-century kitchen, not a scrap was wasted. Stale bread bits were crushed to be used as bread crumbs or broken into chunks to use in savory stuffing or sweet puddings or soaked in liquid to be formed into dumplings. Ever inventive—by necessity and inclination—the eighteenth-century cook knew how to make the most of the ingredients at hand.

Today, with the convenience of commercially made baked goods, why would anyone want to take the time to make rolls, biscuits, scones, and loaves of bread? There are many good reasons! Homemade bread tastes better

and costs less to make; and bread-making is a very pleasant activity to engage in—on your own or, better yet, with your family lending a hand. Bread is also the perfect accompaniment to a simple dinner of soup, makes a great housewarming gift, and is welcome at any potluck gathering. Homemade breads also offer superior flavor and texture, the assurance of healthful ingredients, and wonderful aromas filling the air—so what's not to like? And, the big payoff: the universally loved treat of slathering butter on a piece of freshly baked bread straight from the oven.

Thomas Jefferson's
Sweet Potato–Pecan Biscuits

Irish Soda Bread

French Bread

Cornmeal and Molasses Bread

Sally Lunn Bread

Buttermilk Biscuits

Brown Bread

Parker House Rolls

Cornbread

Hush Puppies

THOMAS JEFFERSON'S SWEET POTATO–PECAN BISCUITS

MAKES 2 TO 3 DOZEN 2-INCH BISCUITS

THOMAS JEFFERSON'S LOVE FOR pecans is well documented and is even evident today when visiting his home of Monticello—some of the pecan trees that Jefferson planted are still alive and thriving. These biscuits are meant to be served as a bread to accompany a meal, but they have enough sweetness that they could even be enjoyed as a dessert.

- 7 cups unbleached all-purpose flour (King Arthur flour is an excellent choice), plus additional for dusting
- 2 tablespoons baking powder
- 1½ teaspoons kosher salt
- 1 cup lightly packed light brown sugar
- 2 tablespoons ground cinnamon
- 1 tablespoon ground ginger
- 1 tablespoon ground allspice
- 1½ teaspoons ground cloves
- 1 teaspoon freshly grated nutmeg
- 1½ cups (3 sticks) cold unsalted butter, cut into ½-inch dice
- 7 ounces (about 1⅔ cups) pecans, chopped
- 3 medium sweet potatoes, roasted (see Chef's Notes), peeled, and chilled
- ¾ to 1 cup cold buttermilk
- Egg wash (1 egg beaten with 1 teaspoon water), optional

Preheat oven to 425°F. Line a baking sheet with parchment paper.

Combine the flour, baking powder, salt, brown sugar, and spices in a large bowl. Add the butter, cutting it in with a pastry cutter (or your hands) until the mixture begins to resemble wet sand. There should still be small but identifiable bits of butter. Add the pecans and mix to combine. Add the sweet potatoes and mix in the buttermilk a little at a time until dough forms a ball. *Do not overmix!*

Dust the work surface and rolling pin with flour and roll out the dough to a ½-inch thickness. Use a floured 2-inch round cutter to cut the dough into individual biscuits. Knead trimmings together, roll out, and cut more biscuits. Transfer the biscuits to the lined baking sheet. (You do not need to leave much room between biscuits, as they rise but do not spread.) Brush the tops with the egg wash before baking if you like.

Bake for about 15 minutes, until the biscuits are golden brown and firm to the touch. Transfer to a cooling rack and serve warm, or cool completely before storing in an airtight container at room temperature. The biscuits will last for 2 to 3 days on your countertop; for a "fresh baked" effect, a quick roast of 3 to 5 minutes in a 425°F oven will heat but not overcook them.

See Season 3, Episode 302

CHEF'S NOTE

❧ **To roast sweet potatoes:** Roast the sweet potatoes the night before you plan to make your biscuits and store in the refrigerator (where they get sweeter over time). Preheat oven to 425°F. Wash sweet potatoes and prick skin with a fork on all sides. Lightly brush with vegetable oil and place on a foil-lined baking sheet. Bake until soft in the middle and oozing, 35 to 45 minutes.

IRISH SODA BREAD

MAKES 2 LOAVES

SODA BREAD IS A quick bread (no yeast required) popular in Ireland. Invented in the mid-1800s, the simple bread uses the most basic ingredients, as they were the only items available to most Irish at the time, indicative of the hardships in that country. It was originally created to bake over an open fire, but you will have fantastic results with this recipe in your modern oven.

- 4⅓ cups pastry flour or unbleached all-purpose flour, plus additional for dusting
- ¼ cup baking powder
- 2 teaspoons baking soda
- 2 teaspoons kosher salt
- 3 tablespoons sugar
- 4 tablespoons cold unsalted butter, cut into ½-inch dice
- 2¼ cups buttermilk (see Chef's Notes)
- ¾ cups raisins, soaked in water overnight and drained (see Chef's Notes)
- 2 tablespoons caraway seeds
- Butter or clotted cream, for serving, optional

Preheat oven to 400°F. Line a baking sheet with parchment paper.

In a large bowl, combine the flour, baking powder, baking soda, salt, and sugar. Cut the butter into the flour mixture with a pastry cutter (or your hands) until incorporated and the mixture is crumbly. Add the buttermilk and mix until combined. Fold in the raisins and caraway seeds.

Dust the worktop with flour and turn out the dough. Divide the dough into two equal pieces and shape each into a round loaf. Place on the lined baking sheet and bake until golden brown and a toothpick inserted comes out clean, about 40 minutes.

Cool on a wire rack to room temperature. Serve with butter or clotted cream if you like. Store in an airtight container at room temperature for 2 to 3 days, or freeze for up to 6 months.

CHEF'S NOTES

- It's not necessary, but I like to **"plump" the raisins** in water overnight, draining them before adding them to the dough. This keeps them soft during the baking process and keeps any exposed raisins from burning.

- **To make your own buttermilk:** Add 1 to 2 tablespoons lemon juice or distilled white vinegar to 1 quart whole milk. Allow to sit for at least an hour in the refrigerator before using.

See Season 6, Episode 605

FRENCH BREAD

MAKES 2 LOAVES

THERE ARE MANY STORIES about how the long, cylindrical shape of French bread came to be. Some people believe that the bread was originally made in a slender shape so that it could easily be pulled into sections by hand, rather than slicing it. Others believe it was shaped this way in an effort to curb knife fighting on construction sites (workers would carry their own knives to cut bread for their lunch and, should an argument occur, use those knives to fight each other). In any case, French bread has become a global classic. This recipe will yield two authentic loaves—I leave the cutting versus tearing up to you!

If you will be making your own sourdough starter, begin that step a day in advance.

- 2¼ teaspoons (¼ ounce) active dry yeast
- 1½ cups warm water
- 1 cup sourdough starter (see Chef's Note)
- 5½ to 6½ cups bread flour (or unbleached all-purpose flour), plus additional for dusting
- 3 tablespoons sugar
- 2 teaspoons kosher salt
- 1 tablespoon oil (to grease bowl)
- ¼ cup cornmeal
- Shallow pan of water for steaming

The night before you want to make the bread, make the sponge: In a medium glass bowl, dissolve the yeast in the warm water, then stir in the sourdough starter. Add 1½ cups of the flour and mix well. Cover the bowl with plastic wrap. Place in warm area and let sit overnight, or at least 8 to 12 hours.

The next day, stir the sponge and scrape it into clean large glass bowl. Add the sugar and salt and mix well. Next, mix 3 to 3½ cups of the flour into the sponge until dough begins to pull away from sides of the bowl.

Sprinkle flour on your worktop and empty the bowl of dough onto it. Knead the dough, adding the remaining flour (½ cup at a time) until it has been incorporated and the dough is lightly tacky but not sticky. Continue kneading until the dough is smooth and elastic. Form into a ball and place in a greased bowl, turning once to coat evenly. Cover the bowl with a damp tea towel or plastic wrap and allow it to rest in a warm place (such as the oven with the light on) until it has doubled in size, 1 to 1½ hours.

Turn the dough out of the bowl onto your worktop (lightly dusted with flour). Punch it down to release the air. Divide it into two equal portions. Allow the dough to rest for 10 to 15 minutes.

Roll each portion into a 15 by 10-inch rectangle. Beginning at the widest side, roll it up tightly, using your fingertips to press the roll down into the flat dough. Once rolled, seal the ends with a pinch. Taper the ends and arrange the loaves on a baking sheet sprinkled with cornmeal. Cover the loaves with a tea towel and allow to proof, doubling in size, in a warm place for about an hour.

Preheat the oven to 450°F. Place a shallow pan of warm water on the bottom rack to create steam. Bake the loaves for about 40 minutes, or until a thick golden crust has formed and, when tapped, the breads sound hollow. Cool completely on a wire rack before cutting.

— CHEF'S NOTE —

❧ **Sourdough starter** can be purchased online, but you'll need to plan ahead as most store-bought starters are only an ounce, or powdered, and you will need at least a cup for this recipe. To augment 1 ounce of starter, add 1 cup unbleached all-purpose flour and 1 cup water the night before using. Blend well and leave the mixture in a covered glass container on the counter overnight.

See Season 7, Episode 709

CORNMEAL AND MOLASSES BREAD

MAKES 2 LOAVES

THE COMBINATION OF CORNMEAL and molasses is a wonderful example of colonial-era cuisine. The ingredients were widely available and were affordable for most colonists. Corn was a hardier crop than wheat, and once it was dried and milled, the resulting cornmeal traveled well. Molasses, a by-product of processing sugar from sugarcane, was readily available and stored well. A myriad of recipes, from simple to extravagant, calling for these two ingredients were recorded in the pages of cookbooks during our early history.

The British have used molasses as a general sweetener in their cooking for centuries. They know it as *treacle*. During the 1600s, when the trade routes between Europe, the Caribbean Islands, and the colonies were firmly established, molasses became even more popular and was used to produce rum in addition to its culinary uses. Cornmeal was, however, a decidedly New World creation. Corn is native to the Americas—the first records of cornmeal date back thousands of years. Cornmeal's coarse texture lends itself perfectly to many styles of cooking, especially baking.

- 1⅓ cups warm water
- 1 tablespoon instant yeast
- ½ cup fine yellow cornmeal
- ⅓ cup olive oil
- ⅓ cup molasses
- 1½ teaspoons kosher salt
- 4¼ cups bread flour (or unbleached all-purpose flour), plus additional for dusting
- 1 tablespoon oil (to grease bowl)

See Season 3, Episode 309

Mix the warm water, yeast, cornmeal, olive oil, and molasses together in a large bowl. Allow the mixture to rest for 5 to 10 minutes to activate the yeast. Add the salt and half the flour and mix well. Once combined, add the rest of the flour (½ cup at a time) to form a dough.

Dust the worktop with flour and turn out the dough. Knead until smooth and elastic (adding more flour if very sticky). Place the dough in a greased bowl, turning once to coat evenly. Cover with a damp tea towel or plastic wrap and set in a warm place until doubled in size, 1 to 1½ hours.

Turn the dough out on a work surface dusted with flour. Punch out any air. Divide into two equal portions. Form each portion into a round loaf by pressing out into a flat circle, about an inch thick. Fold the bottom of the circle up a third of the way. Press the edge into the dough so it does not retract back, and then fold one side of the dough over in the same fashion, then the other side, and then the top. (Do not press the air out of the dough.) Once the folding is complete, flip the dough over and, using your hands, cup the ball of dough and tuck the edges under 4 to 6 times, rotating the ball of dough about a quarter turn each time.

Place each loaf on a baking sheet lined with parchment paper and sprinkle tops with a bit more flour. Cover with a tea towel and leave to proof in a warm place until doubled in size, about 1 hour.

Shortly before the rising time is complete, preheat oven to 425°F and set a pizza or bread stone on the middle rack of the oven if you have one.

Before placing the loaves in the oven, use a sharp knife to cut 4 deep slashes in the top of each loaf.

Gently move the loaves to the hot stone in the oven (or leave on baking sheets if not using a stone). Bake for 45 to 60 minutes, until the crusts are dark brown, firm to the touch, and sound hollow when tapped.

Transfer to a rack and cool completely before slicing.

SALLY LUNN BREAD

❧ MAKES 2 LOAVES ❧

SALLY LUNN BREAD IS a light-textured white bread that is traditionally baked in a Bundt-like pan, which produces a very pretty loaf. This recipe originated in Bath, England, in the eighteenth century and was instantly popular when it was taken to the New World.

The story of the baker Sally Lunn remains a mystery; some even speculate that she existed only in legend form. Whatever the truth, her signature bread—similar to a French brioche—has been enjoyed on both sides of the Atlantic since first recorded in 1780.

- 2 to 4 tablespoons softened unsalted butter (to grease pans)
- 1¼ cups warm water
- 1 tablespoon instant yeast
- ½ cup powdered non-fat milk
- 5 tablespoons sugar
- 2 large eggs, beaten
- 4 tablespoons unsalted butter, melted
- 1½ teaspoons kosher salt
- 6 cups bread flour (or unbleached all-purpose flour), plus additional for dusting
- 1 tablespoon oil (to grease bowl)

Grease two 12-cup kugelhopf (or Bundt) pans with the softened butter.

In a large bowl, combine the warm water, yeast, powdered milk, sugar, eggs, and melted butter. Allow the mixture to rest 5 to 10 minutes for the yeast to activate. Add the salt and then half of the flour; mix thoroughly to combine. Add the rest of the flour, ½ cup at a time, mixing well after each addition.

Dust the worktop with flour. Turn the dough out onto the worktop and knead until smooth and elastic (add more flour if the dough is very sticky). Form the dough into a ball and place in a greased bowl, turning once to coat evenly. Cover with a tea towel or plastic wrap and set in a warm place until doubled in size, 1 to 1½ hours.

Turn the dough out onto a worktop dusted with flour. Punch out any air and divide into two equal portions. Form each portion into a round loaf by pressing out into a flat circle about an inch thick. Fold the bottom of the circle up a third of the way. Press the edge into the dough so it does not retract back, and then fold one side of the dough over in the same fashion, then the other side, and then the top. (Do not press the air out of the dough.) Once the folding is complete, flip the dough over and, using your hands, cup the ball of dough and tuck the edges under 4 to 6 times, rotating the ball about a quarter turn each time.

Once both boules have been formed, poke a hole in the center of each, then gently stretch the hole just enough to fit over the center of the kugelhopf pan and press the dough down into the bottom of the pan. Cover the pans with a tea towel or plastic wrap and set in a warm place to double in size, about an hour.

Shortly before the rising time is complete, preheat oven to 400°F. Remove the towel or plastic wrap and gently place the pans in the oven. Bake until the bread is firm to the touch and hollow sounding when tapped, about 30 minutes. Carefully remove the pans from the oven and place on a cooling rack. Turn the loaves out of the pans immediately and cool completely before slicing.

See Season 6, Episode 602

BUTTERMILK BISCUITS

MAKES 2¼ DOZEN 2-INCH BISCUITS

THE TERM *BISCUIT* CAN mean many things; in Europe, a biscuit is what we consider a cookie. This recipe is a wonderful example of a staple of colonial America, although it is most commonly associated with fare from the American South.

Buttermilk has its own unique story. For as long as butter has been around, so has buttermilk; the acidic milk left behind after churning butter has been used around the world for baking or drinking. In the United States, however, it was only consumed by the poorest of society until the late 1800s, when its popularity as a baking ingredient increased. While some still enjoy drinking buttermilk, this biscuit recipe is the quintessential use for this sour dairy product.

For those who do not want to purchase a carton of buttermilk, you can create a good substitute by adding 1 tablespoon lemon juice to 1 cup whole milk and letting it sit for 5 minutes.

- 2⅓ cups bread flour, plus additional for dusting

- 2⅓ cups pastry flour

- 3 tablespoons baking powder

- 1 tablespoon kosher salt

- 2 tablespoons sugar

- 1 cup (2 sticks) cold unsalted butter, cut into ½-inch dice

- 1⅔ cups cold buttermilk

- Egg wash (1 egg mixed with 1 teaspoon water) or melted butter, to brush biscuits before baking, optional

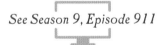

See Season 9, Episode 911

Preheat oven to 400°F. Line a baking sheet with parchment paper.

In a large bowl, stir together the flours, baking powder, salt, and sugar. Add the butter and cut it in with a pastry cutter, or your hands, until the mixture begins to resemble wet sand. There should still be small, but identifiable, bits of butter. Add the buttermilk and mix until just combined. Do not overmix.

Flour a work surface and rolling pin. Roll the dough to a generous ½-inch thickness. Flour a 2-inch round biscuit cutter and cut out biscuits. Fold trimmings together and roll out for more biscuits. Transfer cut biscuits to the lined baking sheet. You won't need to leave much room between each as the biscuits rise up, not out. If desired, brush the tops of the biscuits with egg wash or melted butter before baking.

Bake for about 15 minutes, or until golden brown and firm to the touch. Transfer to a cooling rack and serve warm, or cool completely before storing in an airtight container at room temperature. The biscuits will keep for 2 to 3 days at room temperature or up to 6 months frozen.

CHEF'S NOTE

❧ You can use 4⅔ cups of all-purpose **flour** in place of the bread and pastry flours.

BROWN BREAD

MAKES 1 LOAF

THIS RECIPE HAS A simple name, but the bread it makes is far from ordinary! Closer to a quick bread than a standard bread (because there is no yeast or kneading required), the "dough" is similar to cake batter. And, because it is baked in a traditional, lidded, steam pudding mold rather than a loaf pan, the result is a beautiful bread with a deliciously dense body.

- 1 tablespoon unsalted butter, softened (to grease the mold)
- ½ cup cornmeal
- ½ cup whole-wheat flour
- ½ cup rye flour
- 1 teaspoon baking soda
- ½ teaspoon kosher salt
- ¾ cup buttermilk
- ½ cup dark molasses

Preheat oven to 325°F. Grease a 1-quart steam pudding mold with the butter.

In a large mixing bowl, combine the cornmeal, flours, baking soda, and salt. Stir in the buttermilk and molasses and mix well. Pour the batter into the prepared pan and top with the lid. Place the mold in a deep baking pan. Fill baking pan with water until it comes halfway up the sides of the mold.

Bake for 2 hours. Check bread by carefully removing the lid and testing by sticking a toothpick in the middle. If it comes out clean, the bread is done. Transfer the pan to a rack and allow to cool for 1 hour. Turn out of pan and leave on rack until completely cooled before slicing.

CHEF'S NOTE

- A **steam pudding mold** is traditional, and ideal, for this recipe. If you do not have one, a 12-ounce aluminum can, or any aluminum pan with tall sides is an acceptable replacement; use aluminum foil as a lid.

See Season 7, Episode 705

PARKER HOUSE ROLLS

MAKES 3 DOZEN ROLLS

NEW ENGLAND IS CREDITED with inventing many of the dishes that people associate with American fare. This recipe is not just associated with a region, but with a specific hotel, Boston's famed Parker House Hotel. The simple roll was created in the lavish Parker House kitchens and quickly became a classic, loved by guests of the hotel and by families who enjoyed the recipe at home. This version is the tried and true method for the home cook to make Parker House rolls as they are meant to be.

- 6 cups all-purpose flour, plus additional for dusting
- ½ cup sugar
- 2 teaspoons kosher salt, plus more for sprinkling
- 4½ teaspoons (½ ounce) active dry yeast
- 1 cup (2 sticks) unsalted butter, softened
- 2 cups hot water (120°F to 130°F)
- 1 large egg
- 1 tablespoon oil (to grease bowl)

In the bowl of a standing mixer, combine 2¼ cups of the flour, the sugar, salt, and yeast. Add ½ cup (1 stick) of the butter. With the mixer at low speed, gradually pour in the hot water. Add the egg and increase mixer speed to medium. Mix for 2 minutes, scraping bowl with rubber spatula. Mix in ¾ cup of the flour or enough to make a thick batter. Continue mixing for 2 minutes, occasionally scraping bowl. Remove the bowl from the mixer and, with a spoon, stir in enough additional flour (about 2½ cups) to make a soft dough.

Dust the worktop with flour. Turn out the dough and knead until smooth and elastic, working in more flour (about ½ cup) while kneading. Shape the dough into a ball and place in a greased bowl, turning once to coat evenly. Cover the bowl with a tea towel and let the dough rise in a warm place until doubled in size, about 1½ hours.

Punch down the dough by pushing down the center with a fist, then pushing edges of dough into center. Turn the dough onto a lightly floured surface and knead lightly to make smooth ball. Cover with an overturned bowl and let rest for 15 minutes.

In a 17¼ by 11½-inch roasting pan over low heat, melt the remaining ½ cup (1 stick) butter. Tilt the pan to grease the bottom.

With a floured rolling pin on a lightly floured surface, roll the dough to a ½-inch thickness and cut out pieces with a floured 2¾-inch round cutter. Coat each dough round in the melted butter, fold in half, and seal the edge by pinching with fingertips. Knead the trimmings together; roll and repeat.

Place the rolls in the buttered roasting pan and cover with tea towel. Let dough rise in warm place until doubled in size, about 1 hour.

About 20 minutes before the rising time is complete, preheat oven to 375°F.

Remove the tea towel from the pan of rolls and sprinkle them with a little kosher salt. Bake for about 20 minutes, or until golden brown. Cool on a rack and serve warm.

CHEF'S NOTE

❧ The rolls can be **frozen and baked later**: Make the rolls by following the directions above up until the step where you place them in the buttered roasting pan. Cover the pan tightly with plastic wrap and then foil and freeze until ready to use, up to two months. Thaw overnight in fridge, and bake according to instructions.

See Season 7, Episode 705

CORNBREAD

MAKES ONE 10-INCH ROUND

TO EUROPEANS, *CORN* HAS always been a generic name for all grains, and *maize*, from the Native American *mahiz*, has referred specifically to what Americans know as corn. The colonists associated this native grain not only with the New World but also with the Native Americans (Indians) who introduced them to it; they, therefore, referred to the grain frequently as *Indian corn* to differentiate it from other varieties.

Cornbread was included in period cookbooks, as were recipes for baked and boiled Indian pudding, mush, and Jonny or Johnny cakes, also known as journey and hoe cakes. These mildly sweet (if they were sweetened at all) dishes called for cornmeal, whole corn, or even, as in the case of Thomas Jefferson's "Corn Pudding" recipe, green (unripened) corn. Like this version of cornbread, these recipes were flavorful and quick to prepare. They were frequently served alongside European-inspired dishes on eighteenth-century dining tables, presenting a distinctively American cuisine.

❦ 1 tablespoon unsalted butter (to grease pan)

❦ 2 cups coarse-ground yellow cornmeal

❦ 2 cups all-purpose flour

❦ ½ cup sugar

❦ 2 tablespoons baking powder

❦ 1 teaspoon kosher salt

❦ 2 cups whole milk

❦ 4 ounces lard or 8 tablespoons (1 stick) unsalted butter, softened

❦ 2 large eggs, lightly beaten

Preheat oven to 400°F.

Grease two 8½ by 4½ by 2½-inch loaf pans with the butter.

In a large bowl, combine the cornmeal, flour, sugar, baking powder, and salt. In a medium bowl, combine the milk, lard (or butter), and eggs. Add the milk mixture to the dry ingredients and stir until just moistened. Pour the batter into the greased pans. Bake for 30 to 35 minutes, until golden brown and a toothpick inserted in the center comes out clean.

Cool in the pan for 30 minutes before serving (the long cooling time prevents the bread from crumbling when cut). Cut into squares and serve with butter.

— CHEF'S NOTE —

❦ **Cornmeal**, unlike wheat flour, doesn't contain gluten-producing proteins (which, when combined with yeast, trap gases within batters and doughs, causing them to rise). Therefore, it does not create a light and airy loaf of bread. Although they missed the traditional wheat breads of Europe, North American settlers came to depend on cornmeal out of necessity, mixing it with eggs and water to make fried cornbread and cake.

See Season 1, Episode 104

HUSH PUPPIES

MAKES ABOUT 2 DOZEN FRITTERS

DEEP-FRIED CORNMEAL FRITTERS HAVE been served as part of traditional Southern meals for centuries. The story goes they got their name when cooks would fry fish, crab—or whatever the catch of the day was—outside in the fresh air. Stray dogs would gather around the cooks and bark and howl to get their fill, so it became a custom to fry the batter by itself and toss it to the dogs, saying "hush, puppy!"

- Vegetable oil, for frying
- 1 cup all-purpose flour
- 1 cup cornmeal
- 1 tablespoon sugar
- 1 teaspoon baking powder
- Pinch of kosher salt
- 2 tablespoons buttermilk
- 2 eggs, beaten
- 3 scallions, chopped
- 6 to 8 slices bacon, cooked and diced (½ cup)

See Season 6, Episode 604

Heat 3 to 4 inches of oil in a Dutch oven or deep pot to 350°F.

In a large bowl, combine the flour, cornmeal, sugar, baking powder, and salt. In a separate bowl, mix the buttermilk, eggs, scallions, and bacon. Pour the buttermilk mixture into the dry ingredients. Mix gently, just to incorporate the dry and wet ingredients. The batter should be a bit lumpy.

Drop the batter by tablespoons into the hot oil, being careful not to overcrowd the pan. Fry until golden brown, about 2 to 4 minutes, flipping the hush puppies during the frying process so they brown evenly on all sides.

Remove from fryer and place on paper towels to absorb excess oil. Serve hot.

7

DESSERTS

Tarts, Cakes, Crisps, Puddings, and Custards

avid McCullough, the famed American historian, once noted, "In the eighteenth century, the pleasures of the table ranked high among the pleasures of life." Dessert, the crowning glory of eighteenth-century entertaining, certainly lived up to that description.

The complexity and beauty of many of these historical desserts *are* exceptional—and all the more impressive when one thinks of the typical eighteenth-century kitchen and common cooking tools of the day. Egg whites had to be whipped by hand, as did cream. Creaming butter and sugar together until light and fluffy took considerable work with a wooden spoon. Baking a cake in a beehive oven or open fireplace until the center was done—without burning the outside edges—took practice and skill.

Today, there is a renewed enthusiasm for the "pleasures of the table," and it is reflected in the return to family dinners around the table (*not* mindlessly consumed in front of a television or eaten from a greasy paper napkin in a car!). The tradition of the small dinner party is back, and our passion for cooking from scratch is evident in the enormous popularity of television shows that show us how. And what dinner would be complete without dessert?

There is always a reason to plan a celebratory menu—birthday, anniversary, holiday, family reunion—and that means finishing the meal with a spectacular dessert. But dessert does not have to be so decadent or complicated as to be reserved for a special occasion, as you'll see in this chapter: The Blackberry Peach Crisp, Coconut Bread Pudding, and Coffee Cake, for example, are all easy enough to prepare, but wonderful enough to make your family and friends linger at the table. And later, when the coffee cups are empty, no one feels uncomfortably full.

When there is a special occasion—or a potluck gathering, new neighbor to welcome, or office party for a retiring colleague—you'll find plenty of impressive dishes here to consider.

Apple Tart

Blackberry Peach Crisp

Queen Cakes

Apricot Charlotte Russe

Blueberry Amaretto Blancmange

Chocolate Sabayon with Cognac

Boston Cream Pie

Coconut Bread Pudding

German Chocolate Cake

Coffee Cake

Dutch Apple Cake

Moravian Sugar Cake

Pistachio Financiers

*Candied Mango and
Pineapple Fritters*

Strawberry Linzertorte

APPLE TART

MAKES ONE 10-INCH TART

APPLES WERE CULTIVATED AND used widely by the colonists in the eighteenth century, but recipes calling for apples date back much further: the first recipe on record for an apple tart (titled For to Make Tartys in Applis) is dated 1381. Fourteenth-century versions included figs and were flavored with saffron, and by the eighteenth century, the apple tart was made and seasoned with the spices we use today.

While apples had been enjoyed for centuries in England, it was in the New World that they flourished. Colonists planted European seeds, which grew particularly well in New England and the Mid-Atlantic states, and, through grafting, they quickly bred new varieties. George Washington, Thomas Jefferson, and Benjamin Franklin were among many notable Americans to take an interest in apples, avidly corresponding with European horticulturists and cultivating many diverse varieties in their own gardens.

FOR THE PASTRY

- 2½ cups sifted all-purpose flour, plus more for dusting
- 2 teaspoons sugar
- 1 teaspoon kosher salt
- 1 cup (2 sticks) cold unsalted butter, cubed
- Up to ½ cup ice-cold water

FOR THE FILLING

- 2 Granny Smith apples, cored, peeled, and sliced ⅛ thick (about 2 cups)
- ¼ lemon
- ½ cup dark or golden raisins
- 3 tablespoons unsalted butter, melted
- ½ cup sugar
- 1½ teaspoons ground cinnamon

Make the pastry: In a medium bowl, stir together the flour, sugar, and salt. Using a pastry cutter, a food processor fitted with the plastic blade, or your hands, incorporate the cold butter into the flour mixture until it is a coarse crumble.

Sprinkle the cold water over the flour and butter mixture 2 tablespoons at a time and toss together until a ball of dough starts to form. *Add only enough water to hold the ball together.*

Form the dough into a disc, wrap tightly in plastic wrap, and refrigerate for at least 30 minutes.

Prepare a 10-inch tart pan (preferably one with fluted edges and a removable bottom) with butter and flour: coat all surfaces with butter and then shake flour into the pan until all surface area is covered.

On a floured surface, roll the dough into a circle about ¼ inch thick. Gently roll the dough onto your rolling pin and transfer it to the tart pan. Gently press the dough into the bottom and sides of the pan and trim the top edge as needed. Prick the bottom of the tart with a fork. Refrigerate or freeze for at least 30 minutes.

Make the filling and assemble the tart: Preheat oven to 350°F.

Place the apples in a bowl and cover with cold water. Squeeze in the juice from the lemon quarter. Set aside.

To plump the raisins, place them in a bowl and cover with water; set aside while the oven preheats. Note: You can add a flavor to the water to infuse the raisins. A drop of vanilla extract adds a subtle luscious note.

Drain the apples and raisins. Remove the pastry-lined tart pan from the fridge or freezer. Brush the bottom and sides of the dough with a little of the melted butter. Sprinkle half of the sugar (¼ cup) over the dough, then begin arranging the apple slices in a

shingled spiral or concentric circle. Distribute the raisins over the apples and drizzle with the remaining melted butter. Mix the remaining ¼ cup sugar with the cinnamon and sprinkle over the top.

Bake for 20 to 30 minutes, until the crust is golden brown and the apples begin to gently curl up along the edges. Transfer to a rack and allow to cool for at least 15 minutes before serving.

CHEF'S NOTES

- **Pie dough** freezes well, so I recommend making a double batch and freezing what you don't need. This step will save you time on your next pie.

- I like this tart at room temperature, **served with** cold whipped cream or a big scoop of vanilla bean ice cream.

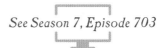

See Season 7, Episode 703

BLACKBERRY PEACH CRISP

MAKES ONE 9 BY 13-INCH CRISP

WHETHER YOU CALL IT a crisp, cobbler, pandowdy, croustade, or buckle, this recipe remains a classic dessert—as popular today as it was for the colonists. In the eighteenth century, this kind of recipe was particularly appealing: baking fruit into a crisp allowed the baker to use blemished fruit, thus wasting as little as possible. While nearly any single fruit can make a great crisp (apples, pears, plums, or berries) one of my favorite combinations is blackberry and peach. Base your own combinations on what produce is in season.

FOR THE FRUIT FILLING

- ⅓ cup granulated sugar
- ⅓ cup packed brown sugar
- ¼ cup all-purpose flour
- ¼ cup fresh crumbs from egg bread (brioche is a good choice), toasted
- 6 ripe peaches, pitted and sliced, skins intact
- 3 pints fresh blackberries

FOR THE STREUSEL TOPPING

- ¾ cup (1½ sticks), unsalted butter, cut into small pieces
- 1 cup granulated sugar
- ¾ cup packed brown sugar
- 1 teaspoon kosher salt
- 1½ cups all-purpose flour
- ¾ cup rolled oats (uncooked)
- 1 tablespoon ground cinnamon
- 1 teaspoon ground nutmeg
- 1½ cups nuts (walnuts, almonds, hazelnuts—your choice), coarsely chopped

Preheat the oven to 350°F. Butter a 9 by 13-inch glass baking dish.

Make the filling: In a large bowl, combine the sugars, flour, and bread crumbs. Add the peaches and blackberries and toss gently to coat.

Make the streusel: In a large bowl, mix the butter, sugars, and salt until only small, pea-size bits of butter remain. Add the flour, oats, cinnamon, and nutmeg and mix until mostly combined. Add the nuts and mix until combined and crumbly.

To assemble: Distribute the fruit mixture evenly in the dish and then crumble the streusel over the top. Bake for about 20 minutes, until the topping is browned and the filling is bubbling. Transfer to a cooling rack and allow to rest for at least 15 minutes before serving. Serve warm, with ice cream if desired.

See Season 5, Episode 506

QUEEN CAKES

MAKES 18 TO 24 LITTLE CAKES

"QUEEN CAKE" MAY SOUND like a large dessert, but this is actually a small pastry. The first recipe comes from the early 1700s and the treat is thought to be named after Queen Anne, whose reign ended in 1714. Now the cake is baked in small, 4-ounce pans, but this feature did not come until the late eighteenth century; prior to that, the recipe had no size specifications.

The fact that Mrs. Goodfellow, owner of a cooking school and shop in Philadelphia, baked and taught this recipe in the late eighteenth and early nineteenth centuries is surprising and a testament to its popularity: In post-Revolution America, there was a major effort to rid the New World of any vestige of British influence in order to establish the U.S. as a unique nation. Despite this environment, queen cakes were baked all over Philadelphia well after the war.

- Softened butter and flour (for the pans)
- 2 cups sugar
- 1 cup (2 sticks) unsalted butter
- 5 large eggs, beaten
- 5 tablespoons heavy cream
- 5 tablespoons brandy
- 5 tablespoons Madeira
- 1 tablespoon ground cinnamon
- 1 tablespoon ground nutmeg
- 2½ cups all-purpose flour

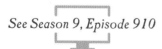

See Season 9, Episode 910

Preheat oven to 325°F. Prepare muffin (4-ounce) tins with butter and flour, coating all surfaces with butter and then shaking flour into the tins until all surface area is covered.

In the bowl of a stand mixer fitted with the paddle attachment, cream together the sugar and butter until light and fluffy. In a separate bowl, whisk the eggs to a froth, then gradually beat them into the butter mixture. After all the eggs are incorporated, beat for an additional minute. Add the cream, brandy, and Madeira and mix to combine.

Sift the cinnamon, nutmeg, and flour over the batter and stir until combined, being careful not to overmix.

Portion the batter into the prepared tins and bake for 15 to 20 minutes, until a toothpick inserted into the center of a cake comes out clean. Cool to room temperature before serving. Store in an airtight container at room temperature for up to one week.

APRICOT CHARLOTTE RUSSE

MAKES ONE 9-INCH CAKE

THE FRENCH WORD *RUSSE* means "Russian," leading many to think this dessert has its roots in that country, but its history is a little more complicated than that. The charlotte russe is believed to have been invented by the French chef Marie-Antoine Carême (1784–1833), who named it "Russe" in honor of his employer, Czar Alexander I. The "Charlotte" is said to be homage to Queen Charlotte, the czar's sister-in-law.

- 3 tablespoons dark rum
- 2 (¼-ounce) packets unflavored gelatin
- 2 cups whole milk
- 1 tablespoon vanilla extract
- 8 large egg yolks
- ½ cup sugar
- 2½ cups whipping cream
- Ladyfingers (recipe follows), or about 3 dozen store-bought ladyfingers
- 1 cup apricot preserves
- 4 fresh apricots, sliced

Prepare an ice bath in a large stainless-steel bowl.

Pour the rum into a small metal bowl and sprinkle the gelatin over the top. Stir to combine. Set aside to let the gelatin soften for 10 minutes.

In a medium saucepan, combine the milk and vanilla and bring to a simmer over medium heat. In a medium bowl, whisk together the egg yolks and sugar. Add a small ladle of the hot milk to the yolk mixture, whisking all the while. Slowly add the tempered yolk mixture back into the milk and

cook over low heat, stirring constantly, until the mixture thickens and reaches a temperature of 185°F on a candy thermometer. Pour the custard into a medium bowl and set aside.

Bring a small saucepan of water to a simmer. Dissolve the softened gelatin into the rum by setting the bowl over the pan of simmering water and stirring constantly until it liquefies. Whisk the gelatin into the custard. Place the bowl of custard in the ice bath and continue to whisk the mixture until it is cool.

Whip the cream to medium peaks in a large bowl. Fold in ½ cup of the cool custard to combine. Then fold in the remaining custard.

Butter a 10-inch springform pan. Lay the 9-inch ladyfinger round in the base of the pan (if using store-bought ladyfingers, arrange the fingers on the bottom of the pan to form a solid base). Next, arrange individual ladyfingers upright, touching one another and forming a solid wall of cake, around the perimeter of the pan.

Fill the ladyfinger-encased pan three-fourths full with the cooled custard. (If you have any custard left over, pour into a freezer-safe container and freeze for another use.) Freeze the charlotte russe for at least 1 hour before finishing and serving.

Spread the apricot preserves over the top, then place the sliced apricots in a ring over the preserves. Carefully remove from springform pan and serve immediately.

LADYFINGERS

- ¼ cup plus 5 tablespoons granulated sugar
- ¼ teaspoon fresh lemon juice
- 5 large eggs, separated
- ½ cup bread flour
- ¼ cup plus 1 tablespoon cornstarch

Preheat oven to 350°F. Grease a 9-inch round cake pan and line with parchment, and line two baking sheets with parchment.

In the bowl of a stand mixer with the whisk attachment, combine ¼ cup of the sugar, the lemon juice, and 4 of the egg yolks (reserve the remaining egg yolk for another use). Whip with increasing speed until thick and light in color. Transfer to a medium bowl and set aside.

Clean and dry the mixer bowl and whisk; add all the egg whites and beat on medium speed until foamy. Gradually add the remaining 5 tablespoons sugar, 1 tablespoon at a time, and increase to high speed, whipping the whites to medium-stiff peaks. By hand, gently fold the whipped whites into the yolk mixture in thirds until 70 percent incorporated.

Sift the flour and cornstarch over the egg mixture and gently fold together until combined.

Spoon 2 cups of the batter into the prepared cake pan. Bake for 7 to 10 minutes, until a toothpick inserted in the center comes out clean. Transfer the ladyfinger base to a cooling rack.

Spoon the remaining batter into a piping bag fitted with a ⅜-inch or ⁷⁄₁₆-inch round piping tip. Pipe at least thirty 3-inch-long "fingers" onto the lined baking sheets. (Keep the lines as straight as possible and approximately 1 inch apart.) Bake for 7 to 10 minutes, until the fingers are lightly browned and firm to the touch. Transfer the fingers (keeping them on the parchment paper) to a cooling rack. If not assembling the russe immediately, store the ladyfingers in an airtight container until ready to use.

Chef's Notes

- Unless you like to bake, go ahead and purchase high-quality **ladyfingers** from your bakery or supermarket. This shortcut will save you a lot of time in the kitchen, but you will still have an impressive and delicious dessert.

- You can make the **custard** a day ahead; store covered in the refrigerator until ready to use.

See Season 9, Episode 908

BLUEBERRY AMARETTO BLANCMANGE

SERVES 6

BLANCMANGE, MADE POSSIBLE BY Arabs, perfected by the British, and given a French name, is a pudding-like dessert that makes one of the most elegant ends to any meal. The recipe dates so far back that the true origin may never be fully known. Because it was originally made with rice and almonds, one of the most agreed upon theories is that it can be traced to its introduction to Europe by Arab traders in Medieval times. But the fact that there are no records of any similar dishes in the Arab world at the time deepens the mystery.

Regardless of its start, by the Middle Ages blancmange was considered an extremely sophisticated dish that was enjoyed solely by the wealthy. It was so deeply ingrained into European culture that it is even mentioned in *The Canterbury Tales*.

- 1 pint fresh blueberries
- 2½ cups heavy cream
- 1½ cups whole milk
- 1 vanilla bean, split
- ¼ cup amaretto
- 1½ tablespoons unflavored gelatin
- 3 tablespoons honey
- ¼ cup sugar

Set a glass bowl (or six serving glasses) on a tray and add the blueberries, distributing evenly. Refrigerate until ready to fill.

In a medium saucepan, combine the cream and milk. Scrape the vanilla seeds into the milk mixture, and then add the pod as well. Heat over low heat until the mixture is just warm and small bubbles appear around the sides of the pan, 3 to 5 minutes. Remove from the heat and let steep 20 minutes.

Meanwhile, pour the amaretto into a shallow bowl and sprinkle the gelatin over the top while gently whisking. Set aside to let the gelatin bloom for 10 minutes.

When the milk mixture has steeped, add the honey and sugar, return to low heat, and stir until the honey and sugar have dissolved. *Do not boil.* Remove from the heat.

Heat a small saucepan of water over medium heat until simmering. Place the bowl of gelatin over the pan to melt, stirring occasionally until it liquefies.

Stir the gelatin into the milk mixture until fully combined to create a custard.

Strain the custard through a fine-mesh strainer into a heatproof pitcher or bowl, then pour into the bowl (or glasses). Refrigerate until set, 2 to 4 hours, or overnight.

See Season 8, Episode 805

CHOCOLATE SABAYON WITH COGNAC

MAKES 2 CUPS

SABAYON IS A DESSERT with deep roots in both French and Italian culture. In Italy, it is known by the name *zabaglione*. The traditional recipe uses egg yolks, sugar, and a sweet wine. In this version, I have chosen to use cognac to honor the French side of the dessert's heritage.

While still considered a lesser-known dessert, sabayon has had a constant presence in American restaurants since the 1960s, although the recipe dates back to the 1800s.

* 7½ ounces chocolate (from 46 to 70 percent cacao is acceptable)
* 8 egg yolks
* ½ cup sugar
* ¾ cup cognac

Set up two double boilers; get chocolate melting over one.

Whip the yolks, sugar, and cognac vigorously over the other double boiler until it reaches 100°F.

Remove the egg mixture from double boiler and whisk in the melted chocolate. Be sure not to drip any water into the sabayon. Whisk until desired serving temperature is reached.

CHEF'S NOTES

* Sometimes **sabayon** is prepared without alcohol of any kind for those wishing to abstain. Espresso can be added in lieu of the cognac or sweet wine, although with an end result quite different from the recipe I have written.

* The **egg whites** that will be left over can be frozen for up to 3 or 4 months.

* The sabayon can also be brought to room temperature, transferred to ramekins, and frozen for a **semi-fredo (similar to a frozen mousse)** pudding dessert.

See Season 7, Episode 704

BOSTON CREAM PIE

MAKES ONE 10-INCH CAKE

THE PARKER HOUSE WAS a true pleasure to explore as we filmed for *A Taste of History*. Boston is a city with a fascinating, rich history—many individuals and events here were integral to the American Revolution. Unlike other desserts that have misleading names, the Boston cream pie was actually invented in Boston, at the Parker House Hotel. The chef, M. Sanzian, who was Armenian-French, created the dessert in 1856 in the hotel kitchen. The kitchen is still in use today, and the "pie" is still a popular item on the menu. As a matter of fact, Boston cream pie is so well loved in Massachusetts, it was designated the state's official dessert on December 12, 1996.

Not a pie at all, the chocolate-glazed, custard-filled layer cake is a remake of the early American "Pudding-cake pie."

FOR THE VANILLA CAKE

- Softened butter and flour (for the pan)
- 4 large egg whites
- 1¼ cups half-and-half, at room temperature
- 2½ cups cake flour
- 2 cups sugar
- 1 tablespoon plus 1 teaspoon baking powder
- ½ teaspoon kosher salt
- 1½ cups (3 sticks) unsalted butter, melted
- 2 large eggs, beaten
- 2 teaspoons vanilla extract

See Season 7, Episode 705

FOR THE PASTRY CREAM FILLING

- 2 cups whole milk
- ½ cup sugar
- 2 egg yolks
- 1 egg
- 5 tablespoons cornstarch, sifted
- 2 tablespoons unsalted butter, cut into pieces
- 1½ teaspoons vanilla extract (or other flavoring of choice)

FOR THE CHOCOLATE GLAZE

- 5 tablespoons unsalted butter
- 8 ounces dark chocolate, cut into pieces
- 2½ tablespoons cocoa powder
- 2 tablespoons dark rum
- ⅓ cup corn syrup

Make the cake: Preheat oven to 300°F. Prepare a 10-inch cake pan with butter and flour, coating all surfaces with butter and then shaking flour into the pan until all surface area is covered.

Beat together the egg whites and ⅓ cup of the half-and-half until frothy and set aside.

Sift the flour, sugar, baking powder, and salt into a large bowl. Add the remaining half-and-half, the melted butter, whole eggs, and vanilla. Beat well for a few minutes, then beat in the egg white mixture until smooth.

Pour the batter into the prepared pan and bake for 30 to 40 minutes, until lightly golden and a toothpick inserted comes out clean. Transfer to a rack and cool the cake completely before assembling the finished dessert.

Make the pastry cream: In a small saucepan over medium heat, heat the milk and ¼ cup of the sugar to a simmer.

Meanwhile, in a medium bowl, whisk together the egg yolks, whole egg, cornstarch, and remaining ¼ cup sugar until smooth. Add the simmering milk, ½ cup at a time, to the egg mixture, whisking continually until fully incorporated.

Return the mixture to the pan and cook over low heat, stirring constantly with a silicon spatula, until the mixture begins to thicken.

Pay close attention to the thickening mixture, and when the first boiling bubble comes through, remove the pan from the heat and whisk in the butter and vanilla.

Immediately pour the custard into a 9 by 13-inch glass or ceramic casserole dish, spread it evenly, and lay plastic wrap directly on the surface.

Refrigerate until the pastry cream has cooled completely.

Make the glaze: In a small saucepan, melt the butter over medium heat; do not allow it to brown or burn. Remove the pot from the heat, add the chocolate, and stir until completely melted. Whisk the cocoa powder and rum together in a small bowl until smooth. Add the corn syrup and whisk to combine. Add the corn syrup mixture to the chocolate mixture and stir to combine thoroughly. Cool to room temperature.

To assemble: Cut the cake in half horizontally. Place the bottom half on a cake stand or plate. Spread the thoroughly chilled pastry cream onto the bottom layer. Place the top half of cake on the filling. Pour the room-temperature chocolate glaze over the cake, allowing it to drip down the sides. Store in refrigerator until ready to serve.

COCONUT BREAD PUDDING

SERVES 8

BREAD PUDDING IS ONE of the oldest recipes that I make on a daily basis at City Tavern. The dessert dates back to the eleventh century in England and has maintained its popularity to this day. Bakers of the Middle Ages and eighteenth-century colonists made bread pudding for the same reasons: to avoid any food waste. Stale bits of bread could be incorporated with eggs and cream and turned into a delicious dish.

Many bread puddings were boiled, which made the process a bit easier—and quicker, as there was no need to wait for an oven to cool to the correct temperature. Other recipes had the puddings baked in a crust. The major flavorings varied from the ever-popular rose water, to grated lemon zest and even vinegar combined with butter. Hannah Glasse's *Art of Cookery, Made Plain and Easy* has three bread puddings, as did Thomas Jefferson's collection of recipes, which also included two sweet butter sauces to accompany them.

This recipe will be familiar to most modern diners as it is a firm, baked custard-like pudding that uses day-old bread in cream. Feel free to experiment, much like our predecessors would have, based on what's in your cupboard. Try sprinkling in any dried fruit instead of raisins. At City Tavern, guests love the seasonal variations, including apricot and white chocolate chunk, blueberry and lemon zest, and coffee and chocolate.

- 1 cup granulated sugar
- 1 cup packed brown sugar
- 2 teaspoons ground cinnamon
- 1 teaspoon kosher salt
- 8 large eggs, lightly beaten
- 2 cups heavy cream
- 2 cups unsweetened coconut milk
- 2 teaspoons vanilla extract
- 10 to 12 cups cubed egg bread (brioche is a good choice), crusts removed
- 2 cups unsweetened shredded coconut, toasted

In a large bowl, whisk together the sugars, cinnamon, and salt. Add the eggs and beat to a froth.

Add the cream, coconut milk, and vanilla and whisk to combine. Add the bread and coconut and massage the mixture together with your hands, breaking up some of the bread cubes while leaving most intact. Allow this mixture to soak for at least 20 minutes (30 to 60 minutes is ideal for maximum saturation).

Preheat oven to 350°F.

Transfer the bread mixture to a 2-quart baking dish, cover tightly with foil, and place in a larger baking dish. Move the whole setup to the oven, then fill the larger baking dish halfway with hot water. Bake for 45 minutes.

Remove the foil and continue baking for another 15 minutes, until the top is golden and there is no custard pooling in the center of the pudding. Transfer the baking dish to a cooling rack and let sit for 15 minutes before serving.

See Season 5, Episode 501

GERMAN CHOCOLATE CAKE

MAKES ONE 10-INCH LAYER CAKE

GERMAN CHOCOLATE CAKE IS a well-known and loved dessert here in America, and many reasonably assume that it comes from a German recipe, or perhaps was just inspired by a German dessert. The truth, however, is that it was created right here in the USA!

In 1852, a man named Samuel German developed a dark baking chocolate for a company called Baker's Chocolate. They quickly began selling his creation as Baker's German's Sweet Chocolate. The German chocolate cake did not take hold until about one hundred years later, when Mrs. George Clay submitted a recipe to the Recipe of the Day section of the *Dallas Morning News*. Her chocolate cake recipe was called German's Chocolate Cake and became quite popular. As time went on, "German's" became just "German."

FOR THE CHOCOLATE SPONGE CAKE

- Softened butter and flour (for the pan)
- 8 large eggs, divided
- 1½ cups plus 2 tablespoons sugar
- ⅔ cup vegetable oil
- 1 cup cold water
- 1 tablespoon vanilla extract
- 2½ cups cake flour, sifted
- 1½ cups cocoa powder, sifted
- 1 tablespoon plus 1 teaspoon baking powder
- 1 teaspoon kosher salt

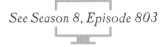

See Season 8, Episode 803

FOR THE COCONUT PECAN FILLING

- 6 large egg yolks
- 2¼ cups sugar
- 2¼ cups (18 ounces) evaporated milk (or heavy cream)
- 9 ounces (2¼ sticks) unsalted butter, cubed
- 2¼ teaspoons vanilla extract
- ⅓ teaspoon kosher salt
- 3½ cups unsweetened shredded coconut
- 2¼ cups toasted pecans, chopped

Make the cake: Preheat oven to 325°F. Prepare a 10-inch cake pan with butter and flour, coating all surfaces with butter and then shaking flour into the pan until all surface area is covered.

In the bowl of an electric mixer with the whisk attachment, whisk together the egg yolks and ½ cup plus 1 tablespoon of the sugar until light and fluffy. Stream in the oil, then the water and vanilla extract and mix until just combined.

Turn off the mixer and add the flour, cocoa, baking powder, and salt. Mix on low speed until moistened. Turn the mixer to high and whip for an additional 30 seconds.

In a clean, dry bowl, whip the egg whites until foamy. Add the remaining 1 cup plus 1 tablespoon sugar, 2 tablespoons at a time, and whip to stiff peaks.

Gently fold the egg whites into the chocolate mixture. Pour the batter into prepared pan. Bake for 45 minutes to 1 hour, until a toothpick inserted into the center of the cake comes out clean or with dry crumbs. Cool in the pan on a wire rack for 15 minutes then turn out and cool completely.

Make the filling: In a large saucepan, whisk together the egg yolks, sugar, and evaporated milk. Add the butter and cook over medium heat, stirring constantly, for 15 minutes, until thickened.

Remove the pan from the heat and stir in the vanilla, salt, coconut, and pecans. Cool the filling to a spreadable temperature before assembling the cake.

Assemble the cake: Slice the chocolate cake horizontally into thirds. Place the bottom layer on a cake stand or plate and spread a third of the filling over it. Repeat for remaining layers. Refrigerate the cake for 1 hour before serving (this time allows the filling and cake to settle together for easier slicing and serving). Stores well in refrigerator for up to one week.

COFFEE CAKE

MAKES 1 BUNDT CAKE

WHEN THE ELLIS COFFEE Company began operations in the 1850s, coffee cakes were just beginning to take hold in America. But it was not until 1879 that they truly stepped into the culinary spotlight. The coffee cake was especially popular in the Northeast and Mid-Atlantic, as the base recipe was very similar to many German and Dutch classic recipes, with a slight American twist.

While commonplace on today's breakfast table, in the 1700s coffee was a thing of great expense and carried the weight of politics with it. Doctors believed coffee would excite nerves and incite people to extreme behavior, including overthrowing governments. Luckily, this concern quickly disappeared and coffee's versatility is celebrated in many forms, such as this delicious recipe!

- Softened butter and flour (for the pan)
- 2 cups all-purpose flour
- 2 teaspoons cocoa powder
- 1 teaspoon ground cinnamon
- ½ teaspoon ground cloves
- ½ teaspoon ground mace
- 1 cup dried currants
- 2 tablespoons chopped candied orange peel
- 2 tablespoons unsalted butter, softened
- ½ cup packed brown sugar
- 1 large egg
- ½ cup strong coffee
- ½ cup molasses
- 1 teaspoon baking soda
- 1 teaspoon water

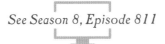

See Season 8, Episode 811

Preheat oven to 325°F.

Prepare a Bundt pan with butter and flour, coating the pan with butter and then shaking flour into the pan until the surface is covered.

Combine the flour, cocoa, cinnamon, cloves, mace, currants, and orange peel in a small bowl.

In a large bowl, cream the butter and sugar until light and fluffy, then add the egg and beat the mixture well to incorporate. Add the coffee and molasses; mix to combine.

In a small bowl, dissolve the baking soda in the water, then stir it into the coffee mixture.

Add the dry mix to the batter and gently fold together, being careful not to overmix.

Transfer the batter to the prepared pan and smooth the top. Bake for about 40 minutes, until a toothpick inserted in the center of the cake comes out clean. Cool on a rack to room temperature. Serve with strong coffee and clotted cream. Store in an airtight container at room temperature.

DUTCH APPLE CAKE

MAKES 2 LOAF CAKES

WHILE THE DUTCH CERTAINLY have created their fair share of delicious desserts, the Dutch apple cake is somewhat of a misnomer. The Germans that settled the New World were often called *Dutch*, a common mispronunciation of *Deutsch*, and at one point the two words were even interchangeable. Despite the confusion, this recipe is decidedly of German roots.

- Softened butter and flour (for the pans)
- 4 ounces almond paste (scant ½ cup)
- 5 large eggs plus 3 yolks
- 1½ cups granulated sugar
- ¾ cup packed brown sugar
- 1 tablespoon kosher salt
- 1 cup (2 sticks) unsalted butter, at room temperature
- 6¼ cups cake flour
- 4 teaspoons baking powder
- 1 tablespoon baking soda
- 2 teaspoons ground cinnamon
- ¼ cup apple cider
- 1 tablespoon vanilla extract
- 3 cups (1¾ pounds) chunky applesauce

See Season 9, Episode 910

Preheat oven to 350°F. Prepare two 8½ by 4½-inch loaf pans, coating all surfaces with butter and then shaking flour into the pan until all surface area is covered.

In a large bowl, beat the almond paste with 1 egg to soften. Add the sugars and salt and mix well. Add the butter and beat the mixture until smooth.

Sift together the flour, baking powder, baking soda, and cinnamon, add to the batter, and mix until combined. Add the cider and vanilla and stir to combine.

Beat the remaining 4 whole eggs and 3 egg yolks together to a froth, then mix them into the batter and beat until smooth. Stir in the applesauce.

Portion the batter into the prepared pans and bake for about 1 hour, until golden brown and a toothpick inserted into the center of a loaf comes out clean. Cool to room temperature before serving. Store in an airtight container at room temperature; keeps for about 4 days.

MORAVIAN SUGAR CAKE

MAKES ONE 9 BY 13-INCH CAKE

IMMIGRANTS FROM CENTRAL EUROPE, Moravians came to the New World in the eighteenth century. The Moravian Church was unique in its outreach to Native Americans and Africans, and the church's communities were known for ingenious self-sufficiency, existing almost completely without external assistance. Their sugar cake was originally only baked once a year, for Easter, but the tradition slowly started to spread to other holidays, especially Christmas, and then throughout the year.

Sugar was mostly available in hard lumps or cones, so recipes often called for "loaf-sugar, powdered and sifted," along with "fine flower, well dryed against ye fire." It would have taken quite a few hours to heat an oven and usually another hour or so to bake the cake.

- 2 cups whole milk
- 1 cup mashed potatoes (1 to 2 medium potatoes), plain
- 1 teaspoon kosher salt
- ½ teaspoon instant yeast dissolved in ½ cup warm water
- Up to 9 cups all-purpose flour
- 2 medium eggs, beaten
- 1 cup sugar
- 8 tablespoons (1 stick) unsalted butter, melted
- ½ cup lard, melted
- 1½ cups (3 sticks) unsalted butter, cut into pats
- ½ to 1 cup packed brown sugar
- 1 tablespoon ground cinnamon

In a large bowl, mix together the milk, mashed potatoes, salt, and dissolved yeast and water mixture. Gradually, add up to 3 cups of the flour in ½-cup increments and mix well. This is your sponge; it should be stiff, but not tough. Cover the bowl with a tea towel or plastic wrap and allow the batter to double in size in a warm place, 30 to 40 minutes.

Add the eggs, sugar, melted butter, and melted lard to the sponge and mix until combined.

Next, work in additional flour in small batches until the dough is blistered and does not stick to your hand. I recommend adding 4 cups flour to start, and incorporating any additional flour needed while kneading on a worktop.

When the dough is smooth and elastic, set it aside while you butter a 9 by 13-inch baking dish.

Press the dough into the greased pan, edge to edge, corner to corner. This may take some time, and if you find the dough wants to shrink back, allow it to rest a few minutes before you continue stretching it. When the dough has filled the pan, allow it to double in size in a warm place.

Preheat oven to 400°F.

When the dough has doubled in size, use your finger to make indentations every inch or two over the whole pan (the more indentations, the more pockets to hold butter and sugar). Push down to the bottom of the pan but try not to make an actual hole in the dough as the butter and sugar may run through it and caramelize on the bottom of the pan, making the cake difficult to remove.

Place a pat of butter in each indentation, followed by a teaspoon or so of brown sugar. Then sprinkle brown sugar over the whole pan, followed by the cinnamon.

Bake in the center of the oven for about 20 minutes, until the top is golden brown and the cake begins pulling away from the sides of the pan. Transfer to a rack and allow to cool before serving. Store in an airtight container at room temperature; will keep for about 4 days.

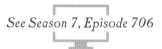

See Season 7, Episode 706

PISTACHIO FINANCIERS

 MAKES ABOUT 2 DOZEN [DEPENDING ON SIZE OF MOLDS]

ALTHOUGH OFTEN MISTAKEN FOR a pastry, this small, delicate dessert is actually a miniature cake. Light and moist, it is very similar in many ways to sponge cake. The cakes were invented in the late 1800s by a pastry chef in Paris known as Lasne. His bakery was near the Paris Stock Exchange and this inspired two major features of his cake: He created the texture so that when it was eaten out of hand, it would not discolor or leave residue (quite welcome to all of the office workers in the financial district). The other feature: Lasne created a pan for the cakes similar in shape to a gold bar, another fitting aspect for his clientele.

Like many of the dry sweets of the eighteenth century, financiers are a cross between little cakes and cookies. Usually prepared with almonds, this recipe is varied to use flour made from pistachios, which Thomas Jefferson cultivated at Monticello for some years.

- ¾ cup (1½ sticks) unsalted butter
- 1⅓ cups pistachio flour
- 1 cup all-purpose flour
- 2⅓ cups confectioners' sugar
- 7 large egg whites

In a small saucepan, heat the butter over medium heat until the solids separate and begin to darken. Remove from the heat and allow to cool completely.

In a large bowl, combine the flours and sugar. Gradually beat in the egg whites and mix until thoroughly combined. Add the cooled browned butter and mix until just combined. Cover the batter and *refrigerate for at least 1 hour before baking*.

Preheat oven to 325°F.

Coat financier molds (see Chef's Note) with nonstick spray (or butter and flour). Fill each cavity three-quarters full with batter. Bake for 15 to 20 minutes, until golden brown and firm to the touch.

Transfer the molds to a rack and allow the cakes to cool to the touch before removing. Serve completely cooled. Store in an airtight container at room temperature for up to one week.

CHEF'S NOTE

- Should you not have **financier molds**, any small and shallow rectangular mold will work nicely.

See Season 8, Episode 807

CANDIED MANGO AND PINEAPPLE FRITTERS

MAKES 30 FRITTERS

PINEAPPLES WERE A SYMBOL of hospitality in the eighteenth century and remain so today. It seems that when a ship's captain returned home from a West Indies voyage, he would place a pineapple on a stick in front of his door as a signal to friends and neighbors that he had returned and was welcoming visitors.

- Vegetable oil, for deep-frying
- 2 cups all-purpose flour
- ½ cup plus 3 tablespoons sugar
- 2¼ teaspoons baking powder
- 1½ teaspoons baking soda
- 1 teaspoon ground mace
- 1 teaspoon ground nutmeg
- 1 teaspoon kosher salt
- 2 large eggs
- ¾ cup whole milk
- 2 tablespoons butter, melted
- 1 teaspoon vanilla extract
- ½ cup candied pineapple, diced small
- ½ cup candied mango, diced small
- Confectioners' sugar, for dusting, optional

Heat several inches of vegetable oil in a large Dutch oven over medium heat to 350°F.

In a mixing bowl, combine the flour, sugar, baking powder, baking soda, mace, nutmeg, and salt. In a separate bowl, beat the eggs, and then add the milk, melted butter, and vanilla. Gently fold the dry and wet ingredients together until just combined (do not overmix). Fold in the candied pineapple and mango, adding enough to make a chunky batter.

Drop heaping tablespoons of batter into the hot oil, 6 to 8 at a time. Fry until golden brown, 4 to 6 minutes, turning to brown evenly. Remove and drain any excess oil on paper towels. Dust with confectioners' sugar, if desired, and serve.

See Season 8, Episode 810

STRAWBERRY LINZERTORTE

MAKES ONE 10-INCH TART

THIS CLASSIC GERMAN DESSERT is in honor of an unsung American hero, Thaddeus Kosciuszko, the general who emigrated from Poland to America to help the Revolutionary cause, showing up on Benjamin Franklin's doorstep in Philadelphia and volunteering to lead the troops. In 1776, the Continental Congress commissioned him colonel of engineers, and in that role his brilliant abilities secured America's forts and rivers against the formidable power of the British Navy. He designed the fortifications at West Point, still considered an ingenious feat of engineering.

He later returned to Poland, but eventually came back to America, settling in Philadelphia, where his house remains a national historic landmark.

As a German-born American, I hold linzertorte very close to my heart; the thin, crispy dessert is normally filled with raspberry preserves and is enjoyed all over Germany and Europe. I have altered the classic recipe slightly by using strawberry jam, in honor of Kosciuszko, who was famous for his love of strawberries.

Colonial cooks made jams to preserve berries beyond the brief season they were ripe and regularly used them in desserts. Also, fresh berries tend to result in a soggy crust while jam gives the tart a chewy center with a crisp, flaky crust. Enjoy this beautiful dessert any time of year and serve it with good coffee, Thaddeus's favorite beverage.

- 1¼ cups all-purpose flour, plus more for dusting
- ¾ cup hazelnuts, chopped finely and toasted
- 1 teaspoon ground cinnamon
- 1 teaspoon allspice
- ½ teaspoon ground cloves
- ½ teaspoon kosher salt
- 1¼ cups (2½ sticks) unsalted butter, at room temperature, plus more for the pan

- 1 cup sugar
- 1 large egg
- 2 large egg yolks
- 1 teaspoon rose water or vanilla extract
- 10 ounces strawberry preserves
- Egg wash

See Season 5, Episode 501

In a large bowl, stir together the flour, nuts, cinnamon, allspice, cloves, and salt and set aside.

In the bowl of a stand mixer fitted with the paddle attachment, combine the butter and sugar and beat on medium-high speed until light and fluffy. Add the egg, extra yolks, and rose water (or vanilla), and beat until incorporated, stopping at least once to scrape down the sides of the bowl with a spatula. Reduce the mixing speed to low and gradually add the flour mixture, mixing just until it forms a soft dough. Wrap the dough in plastic wrap and chill in the refrigerator for at least 2 hours or overnight.

Butter a 10-inch tart pan with a removable bottom; set aside.

Divide the dough in half. Dust the work surface and half of the dough lightly with flour. Roll the dough into a round about 11 inches in diameter and ¼ inch thick. Ease the pastry into the prepared tart pan, being careful not to stretch it, and gently press it into the sides of the pan. Trim any excess from the edges. Roll the remaining pastry into a 10-inch square about ¼ inch thick and cut into ten 1-inch-wide strips.

To assemble the tart, spread the strawberry jam evenly over the bottom pastry. Weave the pastry strips diagonally over the jam to create a lattice. Press the ends of the strips into the edges of the bottom crust, trimming any excess as necessary. Refrigerate for 30 minutes.

Preheat oven to 350°F.

Bake the tart for 35 to 40 minutes, until the crust is golden brown. Set on a rack to cool completely before serving. When the tart is completely cooled, gently remove the sides of the tart pan and place the tart on a serving platter. Serve with whipped cream or vanilla ice cream if you like.

Chef's Notes

- ♥ This recipe is quite **versatile:** You can use another fruit jam (raspberry is a good choice) for the filling.

- ♥ Or make delicate **Linzertorte Cookies:** Simply cut the dough into rounds, then cut out the centers of half of the rounds with a smaller cookie cutter. Spread each full round with jam and place a cut-out round on top. Bake just until golden, about 20 minutes.

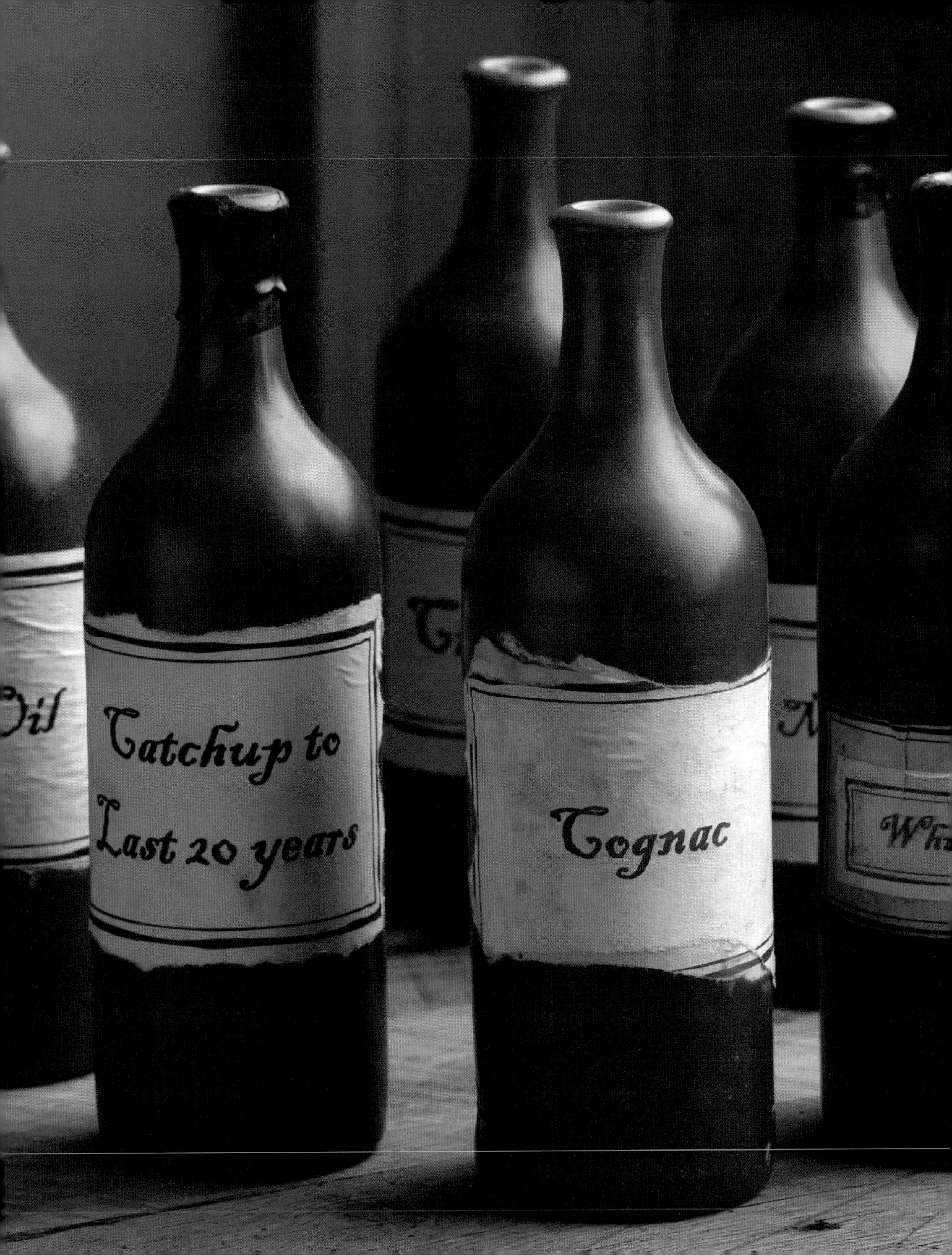
Catchup to
Last 20 years
Cognac

8

PANTRY

Handy Items That Make a Good Cook a Great Cook

Colonial-era cooks did not have freezers; nor did they have the luxury of running to the closest supermarket to pick up a can of chicken stock, bottle of salad dressing, or jar of chutney. So, it's no surprise that research revealed a multitude of recipes for these basics. Most of them are called for in other recipes throughout this book, but you'll find many ways to use them beyond those dishes.

Here is a collection of recipes for a variety of stocks, sauces, and condiments that are handy to have on hand. These made-from-scratch items will elevate whatever you are serving from "This is good!" to "Wow, this is great!" Many of the items can be frozen or stored in the refrigerator for a week or longer; the Chef's Notes will suggest storage tips and variations to the ingredient lists to suit the seasons.

Mayonnaise

Catchup to Last 20 Years

Horseradish Cream

Béchamel Sauce

Hollandaise Sauce

Citrus Vinaigrette

Herb Croutons

Crab Stuffing

Oyster Stuffing

Cornbread Stuffing

Green Tapenade

Mango Chutney

Pineapple Relish

Pepper Jelly

Herb Rémoulade

Demi-Glace

Beef Stock

Chicken Stock

Duck Stock

Vegetable Stock

Court Bouillon

Marinade for Beef, Pork, Rabbit, or Chicken

Jerk Marinade

MAYONNAISE

MAKES ABOUT 1¼ CUPS

MAYONNAISE HAS BEEN MADE since at least the eighteenth century, if not much earlier. The classic condiment can be used for everything from sandwiches to aioli.

- 3 large egg yolks
- 1 tablespoon white wine vinegar
- 1 teaspoon lemon juice
- 1 teaspoon granulated sugar
- 1½ cups vegetable oil
- Kosher salt and freshly ground white pepper

Combine the egg yolks, vinegar, lemon juice, and sugar in a blender or the bowl of a food processor fitted with the blade attachment. Blend on high speed until thick and light yellow in color. Add the oil by pouring in a slow, steady stream, as you continue to blend. Blend until thickened and emulsified.

Season with salt and white pepper and transfer the mayonnaise to an airtight container or serving bowl. Cover, and store in the refrigerator for up to 3 days.

CATCHUP TO LAST 20 YEARS

MAKES ABOUT 2¼ QUARTS

THIS RECIPE IS FROM Hannah Glasse's book, *The Art of Cookery, Made Plain and Easy*, first published in 1745. Even the modern interpretation of the recipe requires a lot of labor and time, but it is included in this recipe collection for curious cooks who may want to experiment with authentic eighteenth-century sauces. It is flavorful and every bit worth the time and expense of ingredients, although it is not for everyone.

This "catchup" is a little more tangy and complex than the usual ketchup you might find at the store. Should you not wish to create this sauce for a recipe from this book, you can substitute fish sauce from an Asian supermarket.

From Hannah Glasse's original recipe:

Take a gallon of strong stale beer, one pound of anchovies washed from the pickle, a pound of shallots peeled, half an ounce of mace, half an ounce of cloves, a quarter of an ounce of whole pepper, three or four large races of ginger, two quarts of the large mushroom-flaps rubbed to pieces; cover all this close, and let it simmer till it is half wasted, then strain it through a flannel bag; let it stand till it is quite cold, then bottle it. You may carry it to the Indies. A spoonful of this to a pound of fresh butter melted makes a fine fish-sauce, or in the room of gravy sauce. The stronger and staler the beer is, the better the catchup will be.

- ❦ 11 (12-ounce) bottles strong, stale beer, such as an IPA
- ❦ 2 (8-ounce) tins anchovy fillets, drained and patted dry
- ❦ 1 pound shallots, coarsely chopped
- ❦ 3 large (about 2 ounces) fresh ginger roots, with skin on, roughly diced
- ❦ 8 cups button mushrooms, hand broken
- ❦ 2 tablespoons ground mace
- ❦ 2 tablespoons whole cloves
- ❦ 1 tablespoon white pepper, cracked

Combine all the ingredients in a large stockpot and bring to a simmer. Cover and let simmer until the mixture reduces by half, 1½ to 2 hours. Remove from the heat and strain through cheesecloth.

Allow the catchup to cool and store in sterile airtight containers, refrigerated, for up to 2 months.

CHEF'S NOTE

- ❦ It is imperative to store the sauce in **sterile glass** jars or containers (not plastic) or it will spoil.

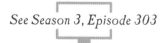

See Season 3, Episode 303

HORSERADISH CREAM

MAKES A GENEROUS ¼ CUP

HORSERADISH WAS AN IMPORTANT ingredient in the eighteenth century. Its distinct tang brought a much-needed brightness and spice into the lives of colonists over the long winter. There are many root vegetables that survive in the root cellar over the course of a winter, but horseradish does not just stay fresh in a root cellar, it continues to grow.

This classic sauce complements the rich flavor of beef. It may also be prepared by whipping the cream, which changes it to horseradish chantilly.

- 3 tablespoons finely grated fresh horseradish (grate on a Microplane or box grater)
- ½ cup heavy cream
- Dash paprika

Stir together all the ingredients and serve immediately.

See Season 1, Episode 106

BÉCHAMEL SAUCE

MAKES ABOUT 1¼ CUPS

THIS SAUCE, ALSO KNOWN as a white roux or white sauce, is one of the mother sauces of French cuisine. It is from this base that you can create a vast array of different sauces, which is why mastering béchamel will expand your repertoire in the kitchen tremendously. As you've noted, many of the recipes in this book call for béchamel sauce.

- 1½ cups milk
- 2 tablespoons unsalted butter
- 1 small onion, finely chopped
- 2 tablespoons all-purpose flour
- 1 teaspoon kosher salt
- 1 whole clove
- 1 bay leaf
- ⅛ teaspoon freshly grated nutmeg
- Freshly ground white pepper

In a small saucepan, bring the milk just to a boil over high heat. Remove from the heat and set aside to keep warm.

In a medium saucepan, melt the butter over medium heat. Add the onion and sauté until softened and translucent, about 3 minutes. Gradually stir in the flour to form a roux and cook, stirring frequently, until well combined, about 1 minute.

Gradually whisk the warm milk into the butter and flour mixture. Bring to a boil and add the salt, clove, bay leaf, and nutmeg. Reduce the heat to low and simmer, whisking constantly, until thickened, about 20 minutes.

Season with salt and white pepper and strain through a fine mesh sieve. Set aside to keep warm for serving; or pour into a jar, cover, and store in the refrigerator for up to 1 week.

CHEF'S NOTE

- Stir 1½ tablespoons **grated fresh horse-radish** into the béchamel to make an amazing sauce for roasts.

See Season 4, Episode 410

HOLLANDAISE SAUCE

MAKES 1¼ CUPS

THIS IS A TRADITIONAL French sauce that many may know from eggs Benedict. Although the ingredient list is somewhat simple, pay close attention to the method. It does take a little bit of finesse, but once you get the hang of it, you will be able to produce this amazing and versatile sauce with ease.

- 4 large egg yolks
- Juice of 1 large lemon (about 3 tablespoons)
- 1 tablespoon dry white wine, such as Sauvignon Blanc
- About ⅛ teaspoon cayenne pepper
- 1 cup clarified butter (see Chef's Note, page 17)
- Kosher salt and freshly ground white pepper

Fill the bottom pan of a double boiler with water to ½ inch below the upper pan and bring to a simmer over low heat. (The water in the bottom of the double boiler should not come to a boil.) Whisk together the egg yolks, lemon juice, and wine in the top portion until light yellow and thick, occasionally removing the pan from the heat to prevent overheating and scrambling the eggs.

Add the cayenne pepper and, in a slow, steady stream, add the clarified butter, whisking until the sauce is emulsified. (Add a few drops of wine if the sauce is too thick.)

Season with salt and white pepper. Serve immediately, while warm.

See Season 3, Episode 309

CITRUS VINAIGRETTE

MAKES ABOUT 1⅓ CUPS

CITRUS WAS AN EXTRAVAGANT indulgence in the American colonies in the eighteenth century because oranges and lemons were imported from Seville, Spain. While it was fresh, citrus would have been used for display on the table, and after it began to age, frugal cooks would have used the fruit for juices and vinaigrettes such as this one.

Vinaigrettes are created by combining an oil with something acidic, such as vinegar or citrus juice. They are used as salad dressings and marinades, and variations of vinaigrettes can be found in most cultures around the world. In the eighteenth century, this style of citrus vinaigrette was popular and even enjoyed by George Washington himself, as mentioned by Mary Randolph in her cookbook, *The Virginia Housewife*.

- ♥ 4 oranges
- ♥ 2 tablespoons red wine vinegar
- ♥ 1 tablespoon olive oil
- ♥ ¼ cup diced red onion
- ♥ ¼ cup diced tomato
- ♥ ¼ cup diced blush (or red) pepper
- ♥ 2 tablespoons chopped fresh parsley
- ♥ 2 tablespoons chopped fresh chives
- ♥ 2 tablespoons ½-inch lengths fresh chives (cut on bias)
- ♥ Kosher salt and freshly ground black pepper

Squeeze the orange juice into a medium bowl. Add the vinegar and oil, then add the onion, tomato, red pepper, parsley, chopped chives, and cut chives. Stir well to combine. Season with salt and pepper. Store in the refrigerator for up to one day, but it is best used shortly after it's made.

CHEF'S NOTES

- ♥ This vinaigrette **pairs exceptionally well** with many seafood and fish entrées.
- ♥ I have added **tomato** to the recipe, which was not commonly used until Jefferson helped make it more popular.

See Season 1, Episode 301

HERB CROUTONS

MAKES 2¼ CUPS

CROUTONS ARE WIDELY AVAILABLE and you will find them on every salad bar, but few people actually make them at home. I hope to change that with this recipe: it is perfect for any skill level, and the croutons will make it impossible to go back to store-bought.

- 4 tablespoons unsalted butter
- 2 medium shallots, chopped
- 3 garlic cloves, chopped
- ¼ cup olive oil
- ½ cup chopped fresh basil
- 3 tablespoons chopped fresh parsley
- 1 sprig fresh thyme, leaves pulled
- 1 tablespoon grated Parmesan cheese
- 12 slices slightly stale white bread (crusts optional), cut into ½-inch cubes

Preheat oven to 300°F.

In a small saucepan, melt the butter over medium heat. Add the shallots and garlic and sauté for 2 minutes, until golden.

Transfer to a large mixing bowl. Add the oil, basil, parsley, thyme, and cheese and blend well. Add the bread cubes and toss until well coated.

Spread the bread cubes, in a single layer, in a shallow baking dish. Bake for 10 to 15 minutes, until golden brown and crisp and dry. Transfer to a rack and cool completely. Croutons can be stored, uncovered, for up to 1 week.

CRAB STUFFING

MAKES ABOUT 2¼ CUPS

CRAB, LIKE LOBSTER, WAS so plentiful in the New World it was used as bait. But it was also popular on the dinner table, prepared in all manner of dishes, including crab cakes, crab soup, and crab stuffing. Crab was widely used by all coastal populations and, in Philadelphia, would have been served with great frequency. Today, this stuffing is a favorite at City Tavern and is called for in some of the recipes here.

- 3 tablespoons unsalted butter
- ½ small onion, finely chopped
- ¼ green bell pepper, finely chopped
- ¼ red bell pepper, finely chopped
- 2 pounds jumbo lump crab meat
- ½ cup fine dry bread crumbs
- 2 eggs, lightly beaten
- 2 tablespoons fresh lemon juice (about 1 small lemon)
- ½ teaspoon hot sauce or Worcestershire sauce
- 2 teaspoons kosher salt
- 1 teaspoon freshly ground white pepper

In a small skillet, heat the butter over medium-low heat. Add the onion and bell peppers and sauté for 5 minutes, until soft and translucent and any liquid they release has evaporated. Set aside and let cool completely.

Pick over the crab meat to find and discard any cartilage and pieces of shell. Transfer the crab meat to a medium mixing bowl.

Add the cooked onion and bell peppers, the bread crumbs, eggs, lemon juice, hot sauce (or Worcestershire sauce), salt, and pepper. Mix well. Cover and store in refrigerator for up to 2 days, until ready to use.

See Season 3, Episode 301

OYSTER STUFFING

MAKES 8 TO 10 CUPS

THIS HISTORIC STUFFING RECIPE, referenced in many antique cookbooks, is a surefire way to impress your dinner party guests or your family over the holidays. Should you (or your guests) not like oysters for any reason, you can substitute sausage for the oyster without reducing quality or flavor.

- 1 loaf firm white bread (about 1 pound), crusts trimmed and bread cut into ½-inch cubes
- 1½ teaspoons olive oil
- 2 onions, chopped
- ½ cup sliced mushrooms
- 2 stalks celery, chopped
- 3 garlic cloves, chopped
- 1 tablespoon fresh thyme leaves
- 1 teaspoon kosher salt
- 1 teaspoon freshly ground black pepper
- ½ cup dry white wine, such as Sauvignon Blanc
- ½ cup chopped fresh parsley
- 1 pint oysters, chopped
- Up to ¾ cup milk

Preheat oven to 350°F. Lightly grease a 3-quart baking dish.

Spread the bread cubes in a single layer in a shallow baking pan and bake for 15 to 25 minutes, until crisp, dry, and golden. Transfer the bread cubes to a large bowl.

In a large skillet, heat the oil over medium-low heat. Add the onions and mushrooms and sauté for 10 to 15 minutes, until golden. Add the celery, garlic, thyme, salt, and pepper and sauté for 5 minutes, until the celery is soft. Add the wine and cook about 5 minutes, until the liquid is evaporated.

Add the vegetable mixture to the bread cubes, along with the parsley and oysters. Mix well. Add enough of the milk to moisten the mixture, but be careful not to make it soggy. Season with additional salt and pepper.

Transfer the mixture to the greased dish and cover with aluminum foil. Bake for 45 minutes. Uncover and bake for about 15 minutes more, until crisp. Serve hot.

CHEF'S NOTES

- Do not be afraid to take creative liberties with this stuffing. For delicious **variations**, try sausage, other meats, or other types of seafood instead of the oysters.

- You can **refrigerate the stuffing** for up to 24 hours before baking, but if you do, you'll need to increase the baking time by 15 minutes.

See Season 3, Episode 306

CORNBREAD STUFFING

MAKES 1 SKILLET

CORN WAS AN INCREDIBLY important staple of the eighteenth-century diet. Not only did corn grow naturally in abundance in the New World, but it also was hearty enough to travel long distances. Wheat flour was incredibly labor-intensive and expensive during the colonial period, but cornmeal allowed bread to be enjoyed in modest homes, at grand estates, and on the battlefield alike. This recipe is a wonderful example of how easy this ingredient is to use: with just a few additions to the cornmeal, you can have fresh bread made over an open fire with no need for a beehive oven, which was required for traditional baking in the eighteenth century.

- Cornbread (page 203), cooled and cut into ½-inch cubes
- 1 tablespoon olive oil
- 2 onions, chopped
- 6 slices bacon, diced
- 3 garlic cloves, chopped
- 1 tablespoon fresh thyme leaves
- 1 teaspoon dried marjoram
- 1 teaspoon dried sage
- 1 tablespoon kosher salt
- 1 tablespoon freshly ground black pepper
- ½ cup dry white wine, such as Sauvignon Blanc
- 4 cups sliced mushrooms (about 12 ounces)
- ½ cup chopped fresh parsley
- ½ cup chopped pecans
- 1 tablespoon chopped raisins
- Up to ¾ cup Chicken Stock (page 265 or store-bought)

Place the cubed cornbread in a large bowl.

Heat ½ tablespoon of the oil in a large skillet over medium-low heat, add the onions and bacon, and sauté for 10 to 15 minutes, until the onions are golden and the bacon is crisp. Add the garlic, thyme, marjoram, sage, salt, and pepper and sauté for 5 minutes, until the garlic is golden. Add the wine and cook for about 5 minutes more, until the liquid is evaporated. Add this mixture to the cornbread in the bowl.

Heat the remaining ½ tablespoon oil in the same skillet over medium-high heat. Add the mushrooms and sauté for 5 to 8 minutes, until browned and the liquid is evaporated. Add the cooked mushrooms, parsley, pecans, and raisins to the cornbread. Mix well. Add enough of the stock to moisten the mixture, but be careful not to make it soggy. Cover and refrigerate for 1 hour.

GREEN TAPENADE

MAKES ABOUT 1¼ CUPS

THE WORD *TAPENADE* COMES from one of its ingredients, capers. In Provence, the caper plant is called *tapenei*. Capers were stored in olive oil to preserve them, and later would be crushed into a paste and used as a condiment to dishes of meat, seafood, or vegetables. Today, we use tapenade the same way, but we also use it as a topping on bruschetta as a savory bite with wine or cocktails before dinner, or as a sandwich spread.

Tapenade can be made with black olives; this recipe calls for green, hence the name.

- 1 cup pitted green olives
- ½ cup finely ground almonds (ground as fine as flour)
- 2 teaspoons capers, drained, with 2 teaspoons of their vinegar
- 1 garlic clove, peeled
- 6 anchovy fillets
- Scant ½ cup olive oil
- Kosher salt
- ½ teaspoon freshly ground black pepper

In a food processor fitted with the metal blade, pulse the olives, ground almonds, and capers. Add the caper vinegar, garlic, anchovies, and olive oil and pulse again lightly. Adjust seasoning with salt and pepper. Transfer to a glass container with a tight-fitting lid and store in refrigerator until ready to use, up to a week or two. Bring to room temperature before using.

See Season 7, Episode 713

MANGO CHUTNEY

CHUTNEY WAS BROUGHT TO America by the British, who had learned to make the spicy condiment from the East Indians. It was a way of preserving a variety of perishable fruits, including mangoes, that were past their normal seasonal prime. Mango chutney would have appeared on tables in Southern colonies, where mangoes grew in abundance. Sarah Gibbons Telfair—the wife of Edward Telfair, a wealthy Savannah, Georgia, merchant who was among those gathered at City Tavern to draft the response to the Intolerable Acts—included tomato, cayenne pepper, and chili powder in her recipe for mango chutney.

When speaking about chutney, I am often asked about the difference between a preserve and a chutney. The primary difference is that a chutney retains more of the texture of the items in it, as opposed to the preserves, which are more commonly pureed and homogenized.

- 1 tablespoon vegetable oil
- 1 medium red onion, halved lengthwise and sliced
- 4 medium fresh mangoes (about 4 pounds), peeled, pitted, and cut into wedges
- 1 red bell pepper, chopped
- ½ cup honey
- ½ cup white wine vinegar
- 1 tablespoon light brown sugar
- ¼ teaspoon freshly grated nutmeg

In a large saucepan, heat the oil over medium heat and sauté the onion until translucent, about 3 minutes. Stir in the mangoes, bell pepper, honey, vinegar, brown sugar, and nutmeg.

Bring to a boil over high heat. Reduce the heat and continue cooking, stirring frequently, for 10 to 20 minutes, until the mangoes begin to disintegrate. Let cool.

Store in an airtight container (preferably glass) in the refrigerator for up to 8 weeks.

CHEF'S NOTES

- It is difficult to predict how long it will take to **cook** as mangoes have many variables that affect cook time such as varietal, size, and age of the fruit.

- To ensure that chutneys and relishes maintain a long **shelf life**, always use a clean utensil when serving, and store in the refrigerator.

See Season 3, Episode 311

PINEAPPLE RELISH

MAKES 4 CUPS

THIS RECIPE COMBINES WEST Indian and Asian flavors, just as they melded in the New World. While most Americans think of pickles when they hear the word *relish*, there are innumerable styles of relishes around the world.

This recipe uses the Antigua Black pineapple, which is similar in color to a Hawaiian pineapple but much sweeter. The skin stays a bright green, even when fully ripe. This pineapple is thought to have been brought over with the Arawaks when they began inhabiting the Caribbean in the seventeenth century. The sweetness of the Antigua Black paired with the acidity of vinegar and the spice of peppers creates a beautifully balanced Caribbean relish that complements seafood or meat.

- 1 large Antigua Black pineapple, peeled and cut into 1-inch cubes
- 1 medium red onion, chopped
- ¼ cup rice wine vinegar
- 1 pinch minced lemongrass
- 1 teaspoon minced fresh ginger
- 1 teaspoon minced habanero pepper
- 1 pinch white pepper

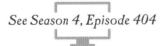

See Season 4, Episode 404

Combine all the ingredients in a medium bowl. Cover and store in refrigerator until ready to serve, or up to 2 days.

CHEF'S NOTES

- Should you not have access to the Antigua Black **pineapple**, any fresh pineapple will work nicely in its place.
- Always wear gloves when handling **habanero peppers** and be mindful to thoroughly wash your hands after using these peppers.

PEPPER JELLY

MAKES ABOUT 4 HALF-PINT JARS

JELLY IS OFTEN THOUGHT of as a strictly sweet item, but there are many uses for jelly outside of sandwiches or morning toast. This jelly provides a nice amount of heat without sacrificing sweetness and makes a good complement to pork and chicken. Apple is one of the core components; it helps provide a little sweetness as well as acting as the binder (the pectin in apples breaks down during the cooking process and provides the texture and firmness of a classic jelly).

Tart green apples have more pectin than sweet apples, so use them here, the earlier in the season the better.

- ♥ 4 pounds apples, unpeeled, chopped into big pieces (including the cores)
- ♥ 3 cayenne chili peppers, sliced in half lengthwise, seeds and ribs removed
- ♥ 1 red bell pepper, chopped
- ♥ 3 cups water
- ♥ 3 cups white vinegar
- ♥ About 3½ cups sugar

Combine the apple pieces (including the cores, needed for their pectin content), cayenne peppers, red bell pepper, water, and vinegar in a large stockpot. Bring to a boil, reduce to medium-low, and simmer for about 20 minutes, until the apples and peppers are soft. Stir occasionally to make sure nothing is sticking to the bottom of the pan.

Using a potato masher, mash the mixture to the consistency of slightly runny apple sauce. (If the mash is too thick, add more water.) Spoon the mash into a couple layers of cheesecloth and suspend over a large bowl. Leave to strain for several hours (even overnight). If you want a clear jelly, do not squeeze or force through the cheesecloth; let it drip. If you prefer a fuller-flavor jelly and do not mind a jelly that is not clear, you can force some of the pulp through. If your pulp is too thick and nothing is coming out, add an extra ½ cup of water. Measure the juice—you want to end up with about 4 cups.

Pour the juice into a large, wide, thick-bottomed pot or Dutch oven. Add the 3½ cups sugar if you have the full 4 cups juice. If less juice, use ⅞ cup sugar for each 1 cup juice. Heat gently, stirring to make sure the sugar dissolves and doesn't stick to the bottom of the pan and burn. Bring to a boil. Cook for 10 to 15 minutes, using a wooden spoon to skim any impurities that rise to the surface. Continue to cook until the syrup reaches 220°F to 222°F on a candy thermometer. The cooking time can be anywhere from 10 minutes to 1 hour or longer, depending on the amount of water, sugar, and apple pectin in the mix.

Pour the jelly into sterilized jars to within ¼ inch from the top and seal. Jelly will keep for up to 2 months in the refrigerator.

CHEF'S NOTE

❧ The recipe makes a mildly hot jelly. If you want a **hotter jelly,** do not remove the seeds or ribs from the cayenne pepper. You can also use your favorite chili pepper in place of the cayenne to make this as hot or mild as you like. I like to use habaneros when looking for some serious heat.

See Season 2, Episode 202

HERBED RÉMOULADE

MAKES ABOUT 2 CUPS

RÉMOULADE IS A SAUCE that has been around for hundreds of years. There are many versions, but this is my personal recipe, and it is the same one that I serve my guests at City Tavern. It is, in some ways, similar to a tartar sauce but much more versatile; this rémoulade is used not just on fish and other seafood, but also on Black Forest ham, asparagus, and more.

- 1 small onion, chopped
- 1 whole kosher dill pickle, chopped
- ½ cup chopped fresh basil leaves
- 2 tablespoons chopped fresh dill
- 2 tablespoons chopped fresh parsley leaves
- 1½ cups mayonnaise
- 2 tablespoons fresh lemon juice (about 1 small lemon)
- 1 teaspoon small capers, drained
- ½ teaspoon Dijon mustard
- ¼ teaspoon hot sauce
- Kosher salt and freshly ground black pepper

In a food processor bowl fitted with the metal blade, puree the onion, pickle, and fresh herbs. Transfer to a medium mixing bowl. Add the mayonnaise, lemon juice, capers, mustard, and hot sauce and mix well. Season with salt and pepper to taste.

Cover with plastic wrap and refrigerate until chilled, about 2 hours, before using. Will keep in an airtight container in the refrigerator for up to 3 days.

See Season 1, Episode 105

DEMI-GLACE

MAKES 7 CUPS

THIS RICH BROWN SAUCE is a French recipe that can be used as a base for many classic sauces. *Demi-glace* means "half-glazed" and is created by combining and reducing a mixture of veal stock and *espagnole* sauce, which is one of the French mother sauces.

- 1 cup (2 sticks) unsalted butter, at room temperature
- ½ cup chopped shallots
- 1 cup sliced white button mushrooms
- 3 tablespoons tomato paste
- 3 cups full-bodied red wine, such as Burgundy
- 7 cups Beef Stock (page 264 or store-bought)
- 3 plum tomatoes, coarsely chopped
- ½ cup chopped leek
- 2 sprigs fresh thyme (or 1 teaspoon dried thyme)
- 6 tablespoons all-purpose flour

In a large saucepan, melt 4 tablespoons of the butter over medium heat, add the shallots, and sauté until translucent, 2 to 3 minutes. Toss in the mushrooms and sauté until any liquid they release has evaporated.

Stir in the tomato paste, then add 1 cup of the wine to deglaze the pan, stirring with a wooden spoon to loosen any browned bits.

Simmer until almost dry, then deglaze with 1 more cup of the wine. Simmer until almost dry again. Add the remaining cup of wine, the beef stock, tomatoes, leek, and thyme and bring to a boil. Reduce the heat to low and simmer for 15 to 20 minutes.

In a medium bowl, knead together the flour and remaining ¾ cup butter to form a paste (*beurre manié*). Whisk this paste into the demi-glace and simmer for 15 to 20 minutes, until the sauce is smooth and velvety.

Line a large colander or fine-mesh strainer with two layers of cheesecloth, set in a large bowl, and strain the sauce. Cool the demi-glace in an ice bath. Pour into an airtight container and refrigerate for up to 1 week.

CHEF'S NOTE

- When **reheating**, add a bit of red wine to the demi-glace and bring to a boil over medium heat. Remove from heat and whisk in 1 tablespoon room-temperature butter per cup of demi-glace before serving to ensure proper consistency and flavor.

BEEF STOCK

MAKES 3 QUARTS

WHILE CANS OF BROTH and bouillon cubes are readily available in all supermarkets, taking the extra time to prepare beef stock from scratch is rewarded with a rich and complex flavor that cannot be replicated with shortcuts.

- 3 pounds meaty beef or veal bones, such as neck bones, shank pieces, short ribs, knuckles, or leg bones with marrow
- 3 cups full-bodied red wine, such as Burgundy
- 1 celery root (celeriac), skin on, coarsely chopped
- 2 carrots, peeled and coarsely chopped
- 1 large white onion, coarsely chopped
- 6 garlic cloves, peeled and lightly crushed
- 2 gallons water, chilled
- 1 (6-ounce) can tomato paste
- 1 leek, trimmed, cut in half lengthwise, and rinsed thoroughly
- 3 dried bay leaves
- 1 small bunch fresh parsley
- 4 sprigs fresh thyme
- 12 white peppercorns

Preheat oven to 350°F.

Place the bones in a large roasting pan and roast, turning the bones once, until the meat and bones are well browned, 1 to 1½ hours. Transfer the bones to a plate and set aside.

Drain the fat from the roasting pan. Add the wine to deglaze the pan, stirring with a wooden spoon to loosen any browned bits on the bottom of the pan.

Increase the oven temperature to 375°F. Add the celery root, carrots, onion, and garlic to the pan, place back in the oven for 15 minutes.

Remove the pan from the oven, and transfer the contents to a large stockpot. Place on stovetop over medium-high heat, and add the water. Bring to a boil; stir in the tomato paste, leek, bay leaves, parsley, thyme, peppercorns, and browned meat and bones; and return to a boil. Reduce the heat to low and simmer, occasionally skimming any foam that rises to the surface, until the stock is reduced to 3 quarts, about 4 hours.

Line a large colander or fine-mesh strainer with two layers of cheesecloth, set in a large bowl, and strain the stock.

Cool the stock in an ice bath and store in airtight containers in the refrigerator for up to 1 week, or freeze for up to 6 months.

CHICKEN STOCK

MAKES 2¼ QUARTS

FOR ANYONE WHO HAS made chicken soup at home, this stock recipe will be very familiar as many of the same methods are used. The stock can be used for a wide variety of recipes, including many within this cookbook.

- 1 (4- to 5-pound) stewing chicken or hen (see Chef's Note), whole or cut into eight pieces
- 2½ gallons water
- ½ celery root (celeriac), skin on, coarsely chopped
- 2 carrots, peeled and coarsely chopped
- 2 medium onions, coarsely chopped
- 1 leek, trimmed, cut in half lengthwise, and rinsed thoroughly
- 1 dried bay leaf
- 4 sprigs fresh thyme
- ½ bunch fresh parsley
- 12 whole black peppercorns, crushed

Rinse the chicken under cold running water and trim off any excess fat. Place the chicken in a 12-quart stockpot and pour in the water.

Add the remaining ingredients and bring to a boil over medium-high heat. Reduce the heat to medium and simmer gently, occasionally removing any foam that rises to the surface, until the chicken is fully cooked, about 30 minutes.

Remove the chicken and reserve for use in another dish. Continue to simmer the stock until it is reduced to about 5 quarts, about 1½ hours more.

Line a large colander or fine-mesh strainer with two layers of cheesecloth, set in a large bowl, and strain the stock.

Return the stock to the pan and bring to a boil over medium heat. Reduce the heat to low and simmer until reduced by half (to 2½ quarts), about 4 hours.

Cool the stock in an ice bath by filling a large bowl with ice and then placing the stock in a smaller bowl that will fit directly on top of the ice. Divide the stock into airtight containers and refrigerate for up to 1 week, or freeze.

CHEF'S NOTE

- **Stewing chickens** (also called hens, boiling fowl, or simply fowl) are usually between 10 and 18 months old and weigh 3 to 6 pounds. Because they are older and larger than roasting chickens, they are more flavorful but also less tender. These qualities make them particularly good candidates for stewing and making rich, golden stock. There is an alternative, though, to cooking a whole chicken. Simply use equal weight of chicken necks and backs, which are inexpensive and full of flavor.

DUCK STOCK

MAKES 1 QUART

THIS RECIPE WAS INSPIRED by my travels to Guyana, a South American nation that is visited by few. Guyana has a diverse populace consisting of Native Americans, Africans, and Spanish and their cuisine reflects this cultural landscape perfectly. Preparing Duck Curry (page 114) is a national pastime for the Guyanese; there is a yearly contest for the best recipe and home cooks from all over the region submit their family recipe in hopes of winning. Duck stock is a wonderful addition to a Guyanese duck curry, but can also be used in any other recipe that calls for stock.

- 3 tablespoons vegetable oil
- Neck, back, wings, stomach, and bits from 1 duck
- 2 onions, chopped
- 3 carrots, chopped
- 3 stalks celery, chopped
- 2 bay leaves
- 3 whole cloves
- 1 teaspoon cracked black peppercorns
- 3 quarts water

In a large stockpot, heat the oil over medium heat. Add the duck parts and thoroughly caramelize on all sides. Add the onions and sweat until translucent, 1 to 2 minutes. Add the carrots and celery and sweat for another 1 to 2 minutes. Add the bay leaves, cloves, and peppercorns to the pot, then add 2 quarts of the water. Bring to a gentle boil and cook until it is reduced by half.

Add the remaining 1 quart water. Line a large colander or fine-mesh strainer with two layers of cheesecloth, set in a large bowl, and strain the stock. Return to the pot, bring to a gentle boil, and cook until reduced again by half, about 30 minutes. Refrigerate in an airtight container for up to 1 week, or freeze for up to two months.

VEGETABLE STOCK

MAKES 2 QUARTS

VEGETABLE STOCK CAN BE easily made at home and provides the distinct richness of beef or chicken stocks without the meat. In many recipes, vegetable stock can be substituted in place of chicken stock without sacrificing any flavor.

- 1 gallon water
- 1 celery root (celeriac), skin on, coarsely chopped
- 3 carrots, peeled and coarsely chopped
- 2 medium white onions, coarsely chopped
- 2 large ripe Roma tomatoes, quartered
- 1 leek, trimmed, cut in half lengthwise, and rinsed thoroughly
- 3 dried bay leaves
- 6 garlic cloves, peeled and lightly crushed
- 1 small bunch fresh parsley
- 4 sprigs fresh thyme
- 12 white peppercorns

Combine all of the ingredients in a large (at least 2-gallon) stockpot and bring to a boil over medium-high heat. Reduce the heat to low and simmer until the stock is reduced to 2 quarts, about 4 hours.

Line a large colander or fine-mesh strainer with two layers of cheesecloth, set in a large bowl, and strain the stock.

Cool the stock in an ice bath and pour into airtight containers. Refrigerate for up to 1 week, or freeze.

COURT BOUILLON

MAKES 3 QUARTS

COURT BOUILLON IS A simple broth that is primarily used to poach seafood, but the classic French broth can also complement vegetables, delicate meats, or even sweetbreads.

- 2 gallons water
- 1 cup white wine
- 3 stalks celery, diced
- 2 large carrots, diced
- 1 large onion, peeled and cut into quarters
- ½ cup sliced leeks, rinsed well
- 2 teaspoons kosher salt
- 1 teaspoon whole black peppercorns
- ½ teaspoon cayenne pepper
- 1 large bay leaf
- 1 lemon, cut into wedges

Place all of the ingredients in a 10-quart stockpot set over high heat and bring to a boil. Reduce the heat to medium and simmer uncovered for about 3 hours, until reduced by about half.

Line a large colander or fine-mesh strainer with two layers of cheesecloth, set in a large bowl, and strain the stock.

Cool the stock in an ice bath. Pour into airtight containers and refrigerate for up to 1 week, or freeze.

MARINADE FOR BEEF, PORK, RABBIT, OR CHICKEN

MAKES 1 QUART

THERE ARE MANY MARINADES available for meats premade at supermarkets, but I have never found a good alternative to this quick and easy recipe.

- 1 medium onion, thinly sliced
- 1 garlic clove, crushed
- 1 small carrot, thinly sliced
- 1 stalk celery, chopped
- 2 tablespoons chopped fresh parsley
- 3 whole black peppercorns
- 1 bay leaf
- 1 sprig fresh thyme
- 2 cups dry red wine, such as Burgundy
- ½ cup red wine vinegar
- ½ cup brandy or cognac
- 1 tablespoon vegetable oil
- Kosher salt and freshly ground pepper

Mix together all of the ingredients in a 4-quart stockpot. Add the raw meat, being sure that the marinade covers it completely, and store in the refrigerator overnight. When ready to prepare the dish, remove the meat from the marinade (discard the marinade), and cook the meat according to the recipe.

CHEF'S NOTE

- For a more intense **flavor**, add rosemary or sage to your liking.

JERK MARINADE

MAKES ABOUT 8 CUPS

- ¼ cup seeded and finely chopped stemmed habanero peppers (about 6)
- ½ cup chopped fresh ginger
- 3 cups finely chopped onions (about 2 medium onions)
- ¼ cup finely chopped garlic (about 6 medium cloves)
- 6 cups finely chopped scallions (about 4 bunches, using white and green parts)
- ½ cup fresh thyme leaves
- ¼ cup freshly ground allspice (not too fine)
- 2 teaspoons freshly ground black pepper
- 3 cups soy sauce
- 3 cups vegetable oil

Place all ingredients, except soy sauce and oil, in a mortar and pestle (or food processor). Pulse to thoroughly combine.

Place in a mixing bowl and add the soy sauce and oil. Store in refrigerator in a glass jar with a tight-fitting lid for up to 2 weeks.

CHEF'S NOTE

- The **jerk marinade** may be prepared in advance and should be kept refrigerated in an airtight, glass container, or clay pot. Do not store in plastic containers as the marinade will eat through the plastic.

ACKNOWLEDGMENTS

Chef Walter Staib

I mentioned in the introduction that there is not enough room to include every recipe from every season in this book. Well, it should come as no surprise that there are innumerable individuals who have contributed to, assisted with, or even accidentally inspired episodes or recipes. In fact, the list of thanks that I would wish to give for a single episode is quite voluminous, and it goes without saying that I will not be able to name everyone. But you all know who you are and I hope that you know my sincere appreciation for your efforts—whether your name is present or not.

First, I would like to thank those who are not only well versed in history, but are also keeping it alive. The reenactors: the people who play the roles of our Founding Fathers to help share their eternal wisdom, and the people who play the everyman characters of the eighteenth century to give a glimpse into colonial life—they are all performing a great service to the public and keeping our traditions where they should be: alive and in person. Among these fine folks, my dear friend Dean Malissa

(the very best George Washington ever, since 1799), Stephen Edenbo (the Thomas Jefferson of today), and the late Ralph Archibald, whose interpretation of Benjamin Franklin is still loved in Philadelphia.

The curators and experts who have shared their wisdom with me and, thus, the public hold a dear place in my heart as well. Susan Stein, curator of Monticello, was instrumental in making the four-part episode a reality; I credit her direct effort greatly with my first Emmy win.

At Mount Vernon, there is Mary V. Thompson, an expert on George Washington and one of the most helpful people you could ever hope to meet. I once asked her a question and she replied with a link to the full-length dissertation that she had written on the subject in question. Amazing! The experience at Mount Vernon would not have been the same without Steve Bashore, the director of historic trades for the estate and contributor to the episode on George Washington's whiskey production. He was kind enough to share his knowledge with the camera and, thus, the viewers at home.

The hosts of the sites all around the world have been truly kind and generous with their time and knowledge and have made me as well as my team feel truly welcome. Whether it be in China, Guyana, or in my backyard in Paoli at General Wayne's estate, Waynesborough, their individual efforts and friendliness helped create an atmosphere where great television is made.

The individuals who have helped actualize my vision are not just at the locations where we film; they are with me every day. Tom Lamb, director of operations for City Tavern, is a longtime employee who is always available to help as needed. My former assistant, Jonathan Jones, played an important role in assisting on the show and was also incredibly helpful with testing recipes. Before Jonathan, there was Miranda Orso and Molly Albertson, and I would be remiss to not mention their diligence in assisting me with my past projects.

There are also people behind the scenes and the camera who made the early seasons of *A Taste of History* incredible. Ariel Schwartz, Jim Davey, and Chris McDowell were the eyes behind the camera at the very beginning, and their talent helped *A Taste of History* evolve into the program it is today. There is also the significant presence of the three people who travel with me behind the scenes, working in the jungles late at night, taking red-eye flights home, and then editing and polishing the content, working more hours than I knew a day had: Thomas Daly, Russell Toub, and Kevin Shaw.

There was also significant contribution from the kitchen: Tony Burnett, my late chef de cuisine, and my former employee chef, Bill Sedermann, assisted with the mis en place and ensured that all prep needed was completed in a timely fashion; a rarity in the world of culinary television! Antonio Jones assisted with the action happening behind the scenes while I am filming, making sure that all the ingredients that are seen on camera are as beautiful and as fresh as possible. My pastry chef at City Tavern, Diana Wolkow, has not only helped with culinary research and general behind-the-scenes activities, but she has also appeared on-screen to help explain her craft to the audience in many episodes.

There were also the figures and organizations that helped from the outside looking in. Ken Hoffmann, formerly with Dietz & Watson, understood my vision from the very beginning and was instrumental in making Dietz & Watson's sponsorship a reality; there may not have even been *A Taste of History* without him. Because of this, I want to extend my heartfelt appreciation to Mr. Hoffmann and the owners of Dietz & Watson—the wonderful Eni family—who have helped make this all possible.

The very same goes for Sandals Resorts, who remain a partner to this day. Gordon "Butch" Stewart—the founder of Sandals—has always seen the value behind my mission and has been by my side throughout this amazing and ongoing journey.

I cannot speak about the Caribbean without mentioning Paul Bauer, a former employee who now works with Sandals Resorts and produces our Caribbean episodes. He was there from day one with my television series and his contributions are sincerely appreciated.

Speaking of the tropics, my journey to Nicaragua was made possible by my favorite PhD in the world—a gentleman who goes by the name of Dr. Patrick Staib. My son not only appeared on these sentimental episodes, but he also contributed a great deal of his time providing research and logistical support for the international filming. I will, however, take credit for his remarkable handsomeness, of course!

While some of the names mentioned thus far may be recognizable to some, there is a name that will be familiar to all, someone who contributed greatly to the success of *A Taste of History*: Governor Ed Rendell. I have been friends with Governor Rendell ever since he was Mayor Rendell, and he has always been a champion of historical education and reenactment in Philadelphia. His efforts within the world of history are a gift to the City of Philadelphia, *A Taste of History*, and our nation in general.

The late Gerry Lenfest—a titan of the communications industry—has been instrumental in the furthering of not just *A Taste of History*, but also American history in general. He was a consistent contributor to my efforts and, through his philanthropy, has also helped to establish the Museum of the American Revolution, my close neighbor in Old City Philadelphia.

While Mr. Lenfest helped make the Museum of the American Revolution a reality for Philadelphia, I would also like to thank the museum's staff, as well. It is complete with talented individuals that—on a day-to-day basis—dedicate themselves to the preservation of history in a spectacular fashion. I would like to thank all of the people that make this possible, of course, but especially Dr. Scott Stephenson. Through his position as president and CEO of the Museum of the American Revolution, he has helped ensure that the founding of our nation will be appreciated for generations to come.

There are many more people who I am fortunate to know and who have helped in some way with this cookbook and none more so than Linda Konner, my literary agent extraordinaire, and the ever-talented Martha Murphy, who helped craft my thoughts and philosophy into the book that you are reading now. I will be forever appreciative of their endless energy and enthusiasm, which kept me inspired throughout the writing process.

There are not just famous names who have provided support; there are many others for whom I owe a debt of gratitude who are out of the public eye. My waitstaff at City Tavern provides visitors from around the world an authentic eighteenth-century experience on a daily basis. My kitchen staff works tirelessly behind the scenes to artfully prepare my historic recipes. There are others off-camera, as well: Aaron White assists with the voluminous research needed for *A Taste of History*, as I have only twenty-four hours in one day and no one person can crawl through the documents alone.

When filming the cooking segments for *A Taste of History*, I most often use my studio kitchen at the Charles Thomson estate, Harriton House, in Bryn Mawr—just outside of Philadelphia. Thomson was the first and only secretary of the Continental Congress, and I consider myself very lucky to be able to prepare eighteenth-century meals in such a setting: the very same in which Thomson would enjoy weekends with his close friend, Thomas Jefferson. But the relationship between Thomson and Jefferson is not the only friendship of note at Harriton House: Bruce Gill, who lives on and operates the estate as a public service, is one of my closest friends. He is a man of innumerable talents and is always willing to share his knowledge with others; fans of the show should recognize the name immediately, as he has been interviewed numerous times. His gracious allowance of using the estate

for filming and his willingness to share his thoughts on camera are not the only contributions: the eighteenth-century plates and dishes seen in this book come from Harriton House's collection and were kindly loaned to me for the photo shoots.

The beautiful photography seen throughout this cookbook is a result of the impeccable talent of Todd Trice. Having known Todd and worked with him on numerous occasions, there was no doubt in my mind that he would perfectly capture the essence of *A Taste of History*. His significant contribution to this project is something for which I am incredibly appreciative, and a simple thank-you does not do it justice!

The National Park Service, with whom I work to maintain City Tavern, has also been of tremendous help throughout my years with *A Taste of History*. My relationship with them has allowed access and support in so many ways that I do not know if *A Taste of History* would be the same without the countless individuals of that wonderful organization.

Much beyond a thank-you, I have saved the most important and personal mention for my late wife, Gloria. It is with her that I took my journey through life, both professionally and at home. We raised two incredible children together, built businesses with each other, and her discerning eye and incessant attention to detail were of monumental importance to everything that I have done. She was the very first and the biggest supporter of *A Taste of History*, and I know that my continuation of this mission is making her smile. For this book, my television work, my restaurant work, and my wonderful life, the most sincere and heartfelt appreciation goes to the one person who was always there throughout: Gloria.

Martha Murphy

Thank you, Walter Staib, for inviting me to assist you in the writing of this book. I've learned more about American history from you than I ever did in school—and it's been a lot more fun! In the process, I've added many new favorites to my collection of recipes.

Thank you, Linda Konner, agent extraordinaire, for introducing me to Walter Staib. You know that cookbooks are a love of mine and being introduced to Chef Walter's television series, *A Taste of History*, was an added treat.

Thank you, Christine Madeira, for jumping in to help format recipes when you were up against a big exam. You are the best!

As always, thank you, Kevin, for being as enthusiastic about this book as I am.

INDEX

ABOUT THE AUTHOR

※━◆━※

Chef Walter Staib is the thirteen-time Emmy Award–winning host of the television series *A Taste of History*, now in its tenth season and viewed in more than one million households nationwide on PBS.

His award-winning restaurant, Philadelphia's famed City Tavern, is a faithful re-creation of the original eighteenth-century tavern that was founded by a group of eminent Philadelphians who believed their hometown deserved a fine tavern reflecting its status as the largest, most cosmopolitan city in British North America. It is located in the most historic square mile in America.

Founder and president of Concepts by Staib, Ltd., a global restaurant-management and hospitality consulting firm, Walter Staib has opened more than 650 restaurants worldwide.

He is the author of six other beautiful cookbooks, five written for adults and one for children.

A James Beard Award–nominated chef and culinary historian as well as a savvy businessman, Chef Staib began his career in Europe, receiving formal training in many of Europe's finest hotels and restaurants.

Walter Staib came to the U.S. from Germany more than fifty years ago with no intention of staying more than one year. Fate had a different plan, and today this proud citizen is an expert scholar of eighteenth-century American history and cuisine, and a self-made master of open-hearth cooking. He has forged an extraordinary connection with American culture and history through food—a story as American as apple pie.

ABOUT MARTHA W. MURPHY, COWRITER

※━◆━※

Martha Murphy is an award-winning writer and editor with a specialty in cookbooks, health, and how-to books. Her writing has been published by regional and national magazines and in twenty-two books that she has written, cowritten, or helped develop. These books have received noteworthy media coverage in publications including the *New York Times*, *Wall Street Journal*, *Boston Globe*, *Baltimore Sun*, *San Francisco Chronicle*, *Chicago Sun Times*, *Houston Chronicle*, and many others. She has been interviewed on National Public Radio and appeared on New England affiliates of all three major television networks (ABC, CBS, NBC) as well as the Food Network.